D1625380

DISCARDED BY
CAPITAL AREA DISTRICT LIBRARIES

THE ART OF
Astrology

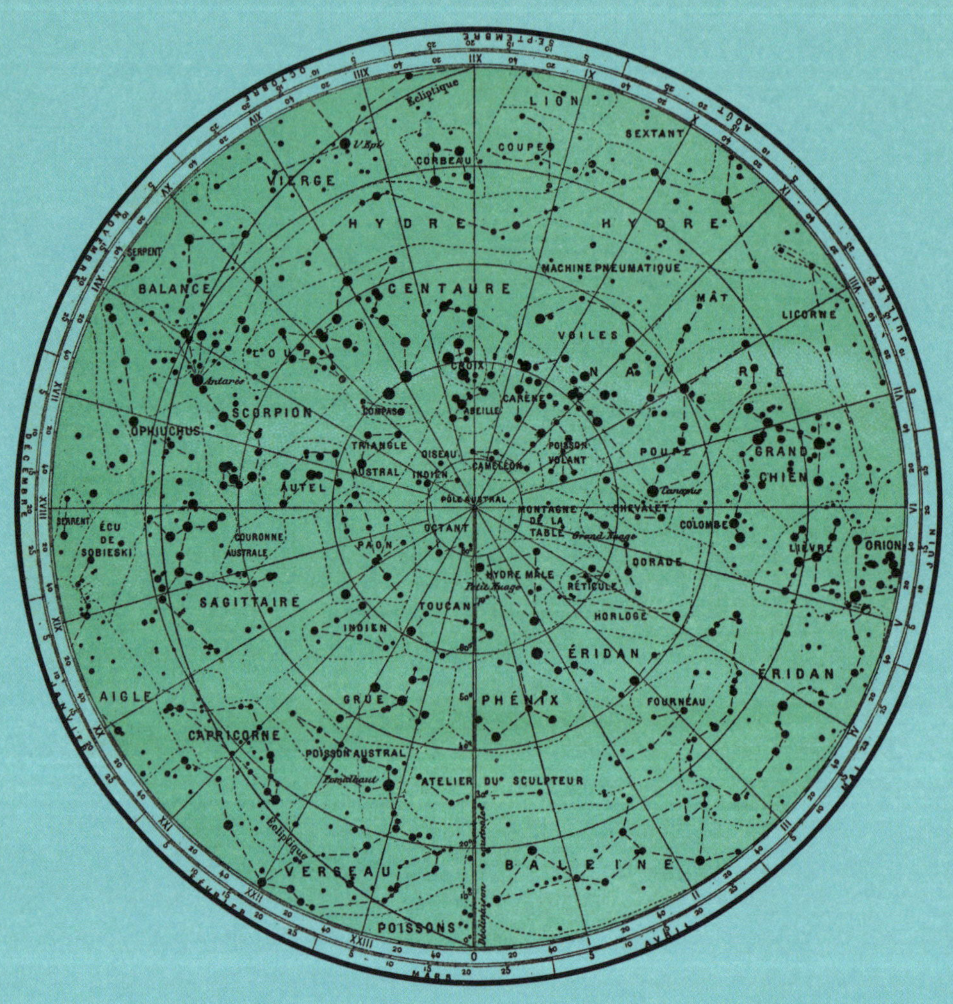
LION
SEXTANT
COUPE
CORBEAU
VIERGE
HYDRE
HYDRE
SERPENT
BALANCE
CENTAURE
MACHINE PNEUMATIQUE
MÂT
LICORNE
VOILES
LOUP
Antarès
CROIX
NAVIRE
SCORPION
COMPAS
ABEILLE
CARÈNE
OPHIUCHUS
TRIANGLE AUSTRAL
OISEAU INDIEN
CAMÉLÉON
POISSON VOLANT
POUPE
GRAND CHIEN
AUTEL
PÔLE AUSTRAL
Canopus
SERPENT
ÉCU DE SOBIESKI
COURONNE AUSTRALE
OCTANT
MONTAGNE DE LA TABLE
Grand Nuage
CHEVALET
COLOMBE
PAON
LIÈVRE
ORION
DORADE
HYDRE MÂLE
Petit Nuage
RÉTICULE
SAGITTAIRE
TOUCAN
HORLOGE
INDIEN
ÉRIDAN
ÉRIDAN
AIGLE
GRUE
PHÉNIX
FOURNEAU
CAPRICORNE
POISSON AUSTRAL
Fomalhaut
ATELIER DU SCULPTEUR
Écliptique
Écliptique
VERSEAU
BALEINE
POISSONS
SEPTEMBRE
OCTOBRE
NOVEMBRE
DÉCEMBRE
JANVIER
FÉVRIER
MARS
AVRIL
MAI
JUIN
JUILLET
AOÛT

THE ART OF
Astrology

A Practical Guide to Reading Your Horoscope

Edited by
ANNA SOUTHGATE

STERLING ETHOS
New York

An Imprint of Sterling Publishing Co., Inc.
1166 Avenue of the Americas
New York, NY 10036

ISBN 978-1-4549-2581-1

For information about custom editions, special sales, and premium and corporate purchases, please contact Sterling Special Sales at 800-805-5489 or specialsales@sterlingpublishing.com.

Manufactured in China

2 4 6 8 10 9 7 5 3 1

www.sterlingpublishing.com

CONTENTS

INTRODUCTION

Astrology's roots are linked to the development of mythologies in early cultures all over the world. Stonehenge, in the British Isles, dates back in part to 3000 BCE, and is thought to have been used to predict the eclipses of the Sun and Moon—events that still have great astrological significance today.

Other ancient monuments for forecasting are found scattered throughout the world, notably in China, India, Japan, and the United States.

The modern, 12-sign zodiac emerged in Babylonia around the fifth century BCE. This system divided the heavens into 12 sections, each consisting of one sign. In the fourth century BCE, Greece became a major center of astrology and as Alexander the Great conquered much of Asia Minor, Egypt, Babylonia, Iran, and India, Greek ideas spread in these areas. Eventually, Egypt became an influential center of astrology and the ideas that developed there formed the origins of modern Western astrology. India and China have separate traditions of astrology that evolved independently.

However, most early astrology, wherever in the world it was practiced, focused mainly on the affairs of royalty and the state; it was only much later that astrologers began to apply their readings to the lives of ordinary people.

▲ Archaeologists suggest that the stone circles at Stonehenge were used as a means of forecasting astrological events such as solstices and equinoxes.

▶ A detail from **The Celestial Atlas**, published by Johannes Janssonius, in 1660–61.

DEVELOPMENTS IN THE WEST

In Western civilization, astrology had been accepted by the Church and the leading philosophers of the time up until the 17th century. In fact, during this time, astronomy and astrology were synonymous with each other. However, its credibility started to decline as scientific thought became more established and various religious movements began to denounce alternative beliefs. As knowledge of the Solar System increased, so doubt was cast on the belief that human life could be influenced by the planets.

SAGITTAR
Corona Auſt.

PLANISPHÆRI
ÆSTUS MARIS PER MOTUM LUNÆ
PISCES
AQUARIUS
ARIES
Triangulum
TAURUS
Andromeda
Pegasus
Equuleus
Delphinus
CAPRICORNUS
Cassiopea
Cepheus
Cygnus
Perseus
Auriga
Aquila
SAGITTA RIUS
Lira
GEMINI
Castor
Pollux
Vrsa maior
Vrsa minor
Draco
Engonasi
Hercules
Serpentarius
Ophiuchus
Corona
Bootes
Coma Berenices
Serpens
SCORPIUS
CANCER
LEO
VIRGO
LIBRA

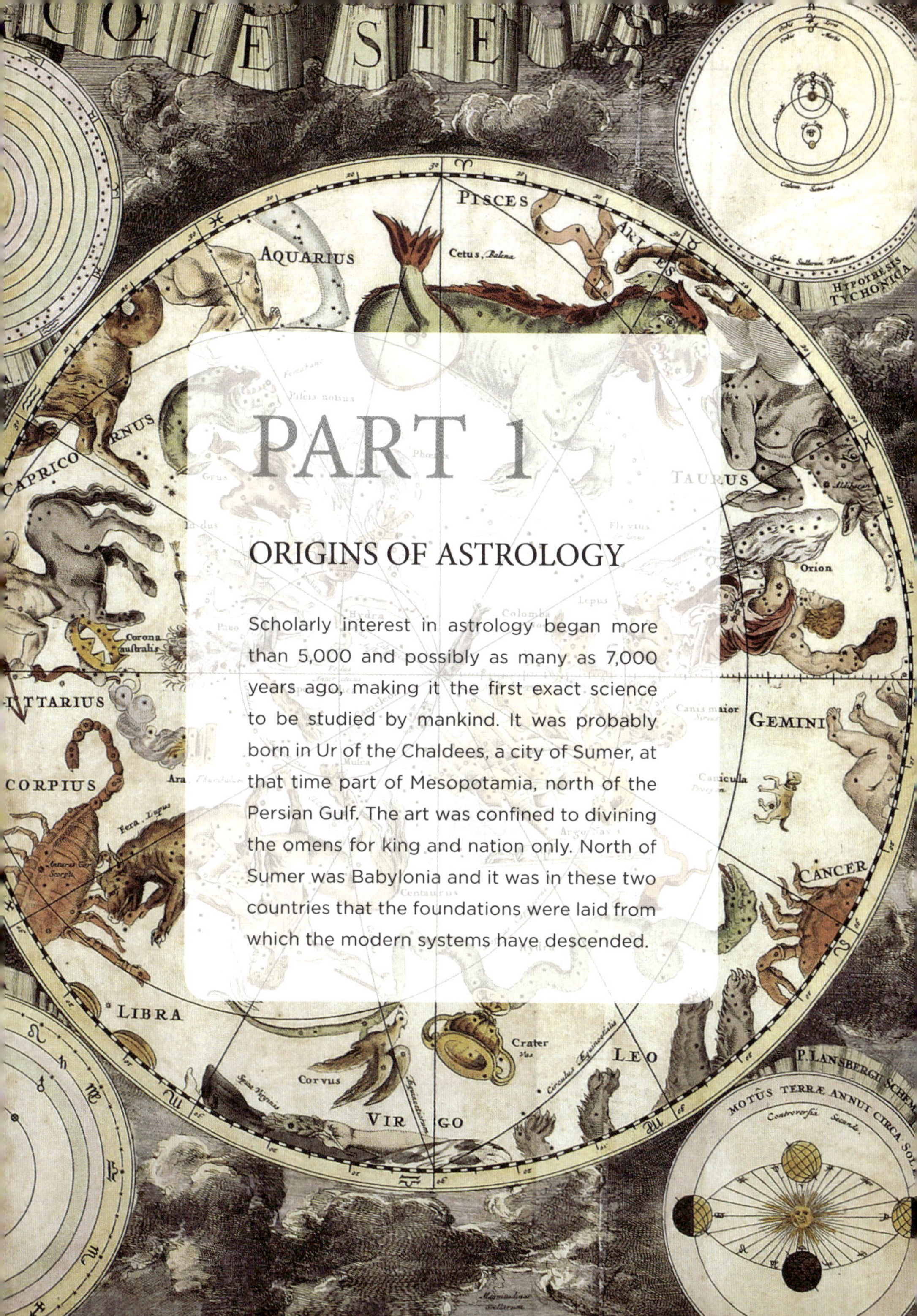

PART 1

ORIGINS OF ASTROLOGY

Scholarly interest in astrology began more than 5,000 and possibly as many as 7,000 years ago, making it the first exact science to be studied by mankind. It was probably born in Ur of the Chaldees, a city of Sumer, at that time part of Mesopotamia, north of the Persian Gulf. The art was confined to divining the omens for king and nation only. North of Sumer was Babylonia and it was in these two countries that the foundations were laid from which the modern systems have descended.

A BRIEF HISTORY OF ASTROLOGY

The fixed constellations seemed unchanging, but in the clear atmosphere of Mesopotamia, where observation was assisted by wide expanses of flat landscape, the movement of those heavenly bodies that seemed to traverse regular paths was noticed, the planets we call Mercury, Venus, Mars, Jupiter, and Saturn were known to the Sumerians and the Babylonians.

The belt of the zodiac in which the paths of the planets mainly lay (though they occasionally wandered outside it, when they were thought to be resting in their "houses") may have been known for millennia, though most modern scholarship ascribes its recognition to Greek science of the sixth and fifth centuries BCE. The Sumerians identified Venus with Innin or Inanna, the Lady of Heaven, and the Babylonians regarded her as Ishtar, goddess of war and carnage in her appearance as the Morning Star, but of love, procreation, fertility, gentleness, and luxury when she shone as the Evening Star. She was the daughter of Sin, the Moon god, and sister of Utu or Shamash, deity of the Sun. Nergal, the Babylonian god of war and destruction, and ruler of the underworld, was appropriately the red planet, Mars; Mercury was Babylonian Nabu; Jupiter was Marduk and Saturn Ninib.

Reports of earthly phenomena apparently resulting from the movements of heaven's gods, though most of them were on the level of meteorological forecasts, were recorded in writings known as the Enuma Anu Enlil tablets, dating from the beginning of the fourth millennium BCE.

Records of predictions followed, first detailing events such as wars and floods, later charting birth horoscopes of individual kings, some of which still exist on cuneiform tablets today.

◀ The Moon and stars feature on this boundary stone of King Nazimaruttash of Babylonia, which dates from the 13th century BCE.

▶ Detail of a celestial map, depicting Virgo. The Babylonians called it The Furrow, and saw it as a representation of the goddess Shala's ear of grain.

Coma Berenices
Vindemiatrix
Virgo
Arcturus
Spica
Crater
XII
XI
180
165
10

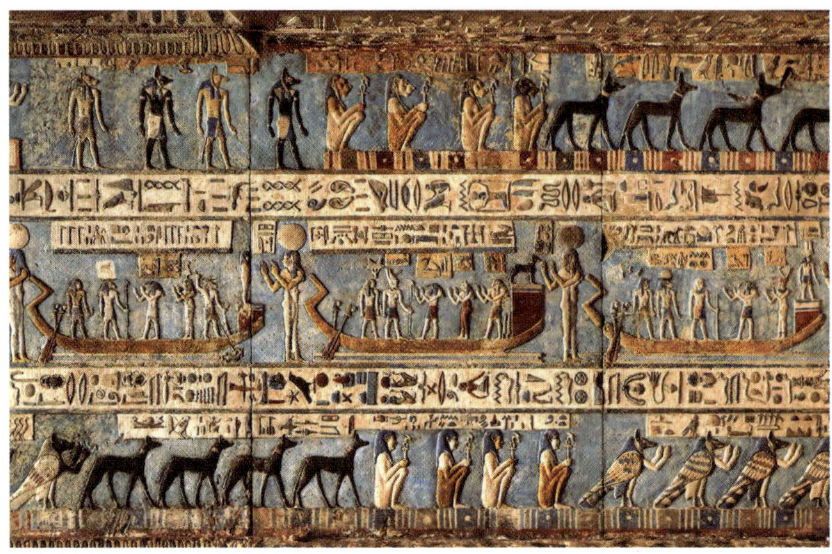

▲ Astrological scenes feature among the hieroglyphic carvings and paintings on the interior walls of an ancient Egyptian temple in Dendera, Egypt.

To the east, Mesopotamian astrology penetrated to India around the sixth century BCE and to China and Indo-China soon after (though there may have been some earlier influence). To the west, it traveled to Egypt and Greece. Primitive peoples in western Europe, independently of Sumer and Babylon, had learned as early as 2000 BCE to mark the solstices and other astronomical events using megaliths. In Mexico, from about CE 300, the Mayas developed a more accurate knowledge of astronomy than the Babylonians, evolving a calendar of 365 days and a zodiac of 13 signs. The Aztecs produced a somewhat cruder system at around the same time.

GREEK INTERPRETATIONS

The Greeks identified the planets with deities very similar in character to those of the Babylonians. Ishtar, the Morning and Evening Star, became Aphrodite, in Roman culture Venus. Nabu turned into Greek Hermes, Roman Mercury, messenger of the gods. Through the conquests of Alexander the Great (356–323 BCE) Greek ideas spread throughout the ancient world, but the Greeks themselves were also exposed to foreign influence. In 280 BCE Berosus, a Chaldean priest, brought astrology to Greece.

EGYPTIAN ASTRONOMY

Egypt developed its own astronomy. From possibly 2000 BCE it was using a calendar that the Greeks later made their own. The Persians introduced astrology to Egypt in the sixth century BCE, with the result that the Egyptians evolved a form of astral

▲ Reliefs from the White Cloud Temple, a Taoist temple in southern Beijing, China, depicting the Chinese zodiacal signs of the tiger and the ox.

religion that eventually influenced both Greece and Rome. Thirty-six stars named "decans" were selected, rising at ten-day intervals, each governed by a spirit. The ten-day periods evolved into ten-degree subdivisions of the twelve 30° zodiacal signs. In about 150 BCE a treatise by a fictitious priest, Petosiris, and king, Nechepso, ascribed each day of the week to a planet. Even more important was the collection of texts made between 50 BCE and CE 150, attributed to Hermes, the Greek Mercury and Egyptian Thoth.

THE CHINESE ZODIAC

The Chinese were probably the first people to develop astronomy apart from astrology, which they used to forecast events. They divided the sky into five "palaces," a central region around the pole and four equatorial divisions corresponding to the four seasons. Twelve signs—Tiger, Rabbit, Dragon, Serpent, Horse, Sheep, Monkey, Hen, Dog, Pig, Rat, and Ox—alternatively possessing the quality of positive *Yang* (masculinity, light, and motion) and negative *Yin* (femininity, darkness, and repose), were based on divisions of the Equator (not of the sky, as with the zodiac).

DEVELOPMENTS IN EUROPE

The complicated and apparently scientific system that was to be the ancestor of European astrology was meanwhile being developed by the Greeks from their own genius combined with Babylonian and Egyptian elements. Philosophy, medicine, and religion all supported it. The

Stoic doctrine of universal "sympathy" between the microcosm (man) and the macrocosm (the Universe)—expressed in the dictum used later when Stoicism no longer existed, "as above, so below"—and astrology seemed made for each other. Mithraism, a rival of Christianity, initiated its worshipers, who in their rites wore masks representing the animals of the zodiac, into successive mysteries representing the soul's journey through the seven planetary realms. Gnosticism in its many forms and some of the mystery religions were based on very similar concepts. Melothesis, a "science" in which the stars and zodiac dominate parts of the body, became part of standard medical practice.

In Rome the official augurs opposed astrology when it arrived there during the second century BCE, but the populace welcomed "Chaldeans" who told their fortunes by the stars. The Roman emperors disliked astrology, regarding it as a possible weapon to be used by would-be usurpers of their thrones. It found a supporter in the person of the Neoplatonist philosopher Plotinus, who settled in Rome in CE 241.

Early Christianity was sometimes tolerant of, sometimes hostile to, astrology. The Clementine Recognitions (second century) stated that God created the celestial bodies to be an indication of things past, present, and future and that Abraham had recognized the creator from the stars. Hostile Christian writers, including Augustine, attacked astrology

▼ Ptolemy (Claudius Ptolemaeus) established the theory accepted until the 15th century that the Earth was the center of the Universe.

SCORPION PHÉNIX FOURNEAU GRUE

with a double-edged sword of an argument—it was either erroneous or, if right, owed its accuracy to the devil.

ASTROLOGY AND JUDAISM

Judaism generally had little time for astrology, even though it recorded the fact that "the stars in their courses fought against" Sisera. According to Christianity, Judaism's largest and most successful heresy, the coming of Christ, broke the control of the planets over human fate. One Christian view was that the star of Bethlehem changed the old order; another that it was the constellation of Cassiopeia, which produced an unusually bright star every 300 years and was known to the ancients as "The Woman with Child." Furthermore, Cassiopeia was the presiding constellation of Syria/Palestine, and it was natural for the Magi, who were astrologers, not kings, to follow the sign that proclaimed to them that a woman of Palestine had brought forth a royal son.

The Jewish *Sefer Yetzirah* (Book of Creation, written ca CE 500)—also known as the *Kabbalah*—and *Zohar* (Book of Splendor) both affected European thought. They also revealed faith in celestial influence.

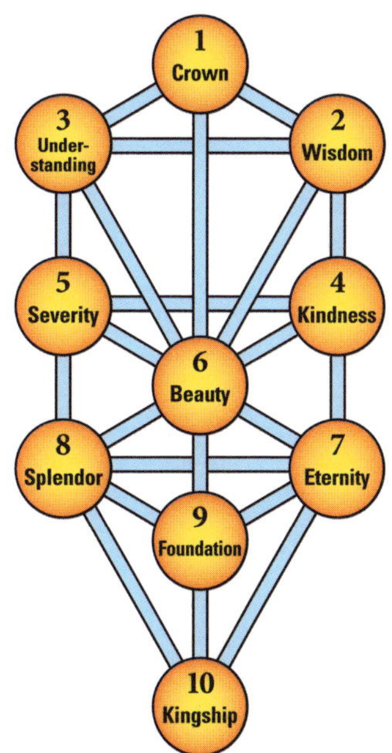

▲ At the heart of the Jewish Kabbalah are the Ten Sefirot. Also known as the Tree of Life, this system attempts to explain the origins of the Universe.

TOWARD ACCEPTANCE

During the Dark Ages, astrology was kept alive by the Mohammedans. In the eighth century the Caliph Al-Mansur founded a school of astrology in Baghdad with the practical aims of catching thieves, recovering lost possessions, and determining the best time to start enterprises. When learning revived in the 11th and 12th centuries Christendom accepted Arabian astrological treatises because of their Aristotelian flavor. Aquinas (ca 1225–1274) gave the definitive Christian compromise with astrology and made it acceptable. Since the stars influence human appetites, which few men can resist, their forecasts are mostly correct; but those morally strong enough to resist can negate their predictions. The interest in astrology reached its zenith during the Renaissance. Famous scholars wrote treatises, of whom the most eminent was the Swiss Paracelsus (1493–1541) who believed that man's inner nature corresponded to the Universe.

WESTERN ASTROLOGY

At the moment of your birth, the Sun, Moon, and eight planets were at precise positions in the sky. They were in the same segments of the sky as various of the 12 particular constellations of stars that make up the zodiac. The strengths and weaknesses of your personality and some of the major events in your life were predetermined by these astronomical positions. This is the basis of the complex science of astrology.

THE ZODIAC

The zodiac is a relatively narrow band of stars (about 18° wide) against which the Sun, Moon, and planets move. It stretches right around the Earth and its 360° have been divided up into 12 equal segments of 30°. These segments are named after 12 constellations of stars that more or less occupy parts of the segments. The constellations correspond to the 12 signs of the zodiac. Note that the central line of the zodiac is known as the "ecliptic."

A BRIEF HISTORY

It is important to remember that astrology was the same thing as astronomy from Babylonian times through the refinement of techniques by the Greeks, Romans, and early medieval Arabs. The early Christians, among them St. Augustine, attacked astrology, and it was in decline in western Europe for about 800 years.

Only in the 17th century, when the first modern astronomers appeared, did astronomy split away from astrology. At the same time, there was increased interest in astrology, especially in England, and much of the complex detail was worked out by men such as John Dee (astrologer to Queen Elizabeth I); William Lilly, who in 1648 in his *Astrological Predictions* forecast "sundry fires and consuming plague" for London in about 1665 (he was correct, since the Great Plague was in 1665 and the Fire of London in 1666); Francis Moore (whose *Vox Stellarum* became *Old Moore's Almanac*, still published each year); and Ebenezer Sibly who, in 1784, produced *The Celestial Science of Astrology*, the most complete and ambitious work on the subject up to that date.

Until 1931, astrological prediction had tended to be based on personal horoscopes (birth charts that showed the sky at the moment of birth, with the Earth in the center surrounded by the planets and constellations). Essentially, they were produced privately by an astrologer for a client. On August 24, 1931, Princess Margaret was born to the Duke and Duchess of York and the *Sunday Express* published a birth chart of the baby. This led to a sudden rekindling of interest in astrological predictions in several newspapers as a regular feature.

▶ The birth charts of the French monarch Louis XVI and his wife, Marie Antoinette, dated 1795.

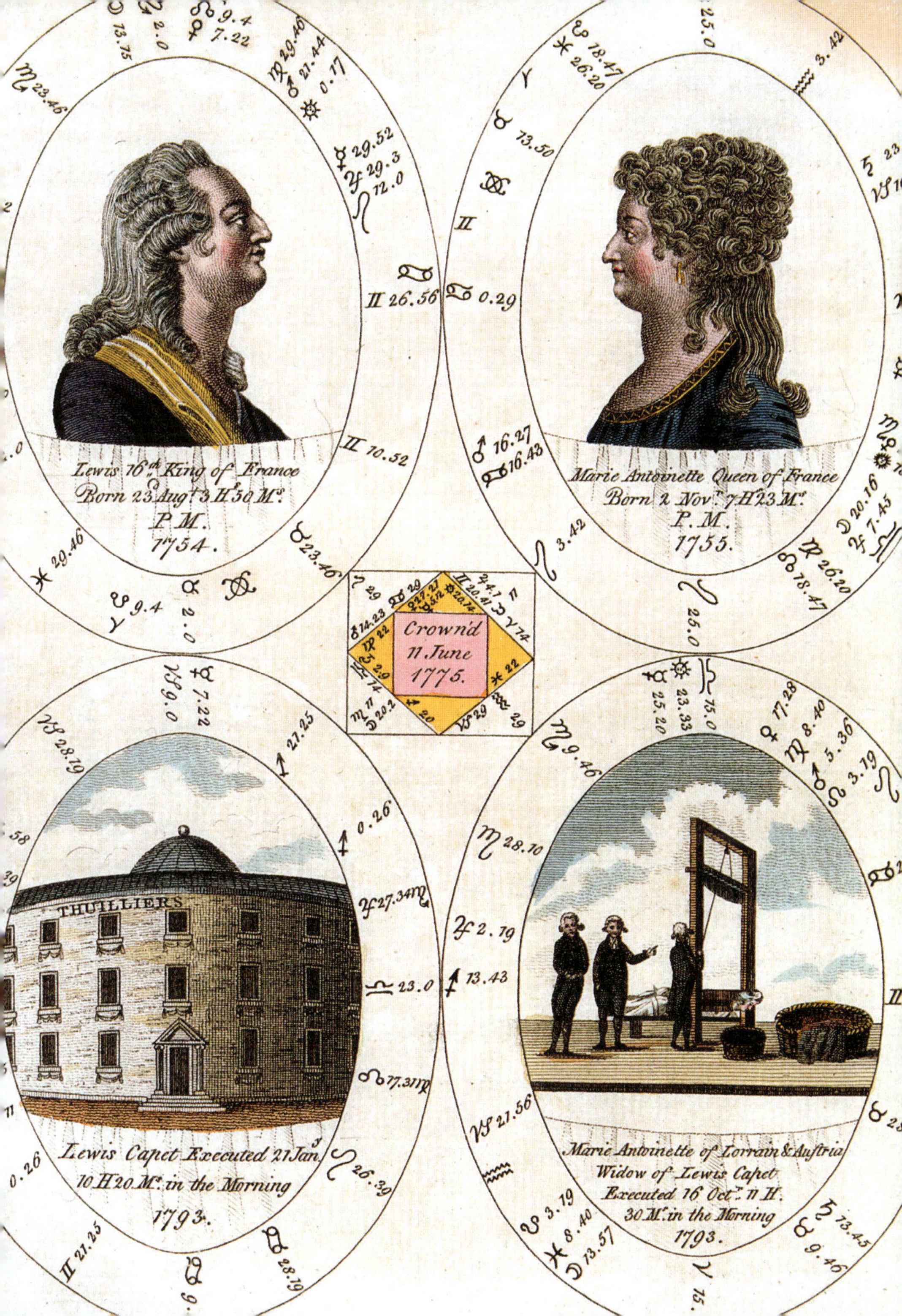
Lewis 16th King of France
Born 23 Augt 3 H 30 Ms.
P. M.
1754.
Marie Antoinette Queen of France
Born 2 Novr. 7 H 23 Ms.
P. M.
1755.
Crown'd
11. June
1775.
THUILLIERS
Lewis Capet Executed 21 Jan.
10 H 20 Ms. in the Morning
1793.
Marie Antoinette of Lorrain & Austria
Widow of Lewis Capet
Executed 16 Octr. 11 H.
30 Ms. in the Morning
1793.

CALCULATING A PERSONAL BIRTH CHART

It is a complex task to calculate a personal birth chart. Only a brief outline of the procedure is given here so that you can appreciate some of the difficulties involved. The basic equipment needed are a pair of compasses, a pencil, a protractor, an atlas that lists latitudes and longitudes of places around the world, and (the difficult part) an "ephemeris," which is a book giving the positions of the Sun, Moon, and planets at particular times.

Ideally, you should draw two separate disks, one of which fits around the other. The outer disk (*see* below) needs to be divided into 30° segments inscribed with the 12 signs of the zodiac, proceeding counterclockwise from Aries through to Pisces. The inner disk (*see* opposite) has the Earth at its center. It is really a diagram of the sky, showing north, south, east, and west, but reversed from normal maps, with east to the left. Also, it shows times, with dawn (6 A.M.) to the east (this is known as the "ascendant" and is very important), noon to the south (at the top of the diagram, a position also known as Medium Coeli or Midheaven), dusk to the west, and midnight (Imum Coeli) to the north.

Another feature of the basic diagram is the array of houses. These have no astronomical significance but are important in the analysis of fortune from the chart. There are a total of 12 houses, arranged around the inner ring, going counterclockwise from the ascendant.

The divisions between the houses and between the zodiacal signs are known as "cusps." The cusp of a particular house or sign is at its starting point. So the cusp of the first house is on the ascendant. House and sign cusps will not usually coincide. Cusps are important, because a planet close to one will be affected by the houses or signs to either side of the cusp, and so any prediction needs to be amended.

To illustrate some of the difficulties of casting a birth chart, here are the time adjustments needed. If you know your time of birth to the nearest minute you must then proceed as follows:

▲ The outer disk: Once the inner disk is placed over the top of this, just the signs of the zodiac are visible.

- Correct your time of birth to Greenwich Mean Time (GMT) by adding the time difference if you were born to the west of Greenwich (if you were born in New York, add five hours), or by subtracting the time difference if you were born to the east of Greenwich (if you were born in Queensland, Australia, subtract ten hours). If you were born in Britain or elsewhere on the Greenwich meridian, the GMT time zone covers you and no adjustment for longitude is necessary.
- Having found the sidereal time of your birth, now look up the positions of the Sun, Moon, and planets at that time (or adjust it from noon data). You will be able to set the ascendant on your birth chart to the correct number of degrees of the correct sign, then fasten the two separate disks together, and fill in the rest of the data. If you were born after midday, you will need to add (or if before midday, subtract) a further allowance.
- Make an allowance for any daylight saving time—that hour or occasionally more, by which some countries advance their clocks during the summer months.

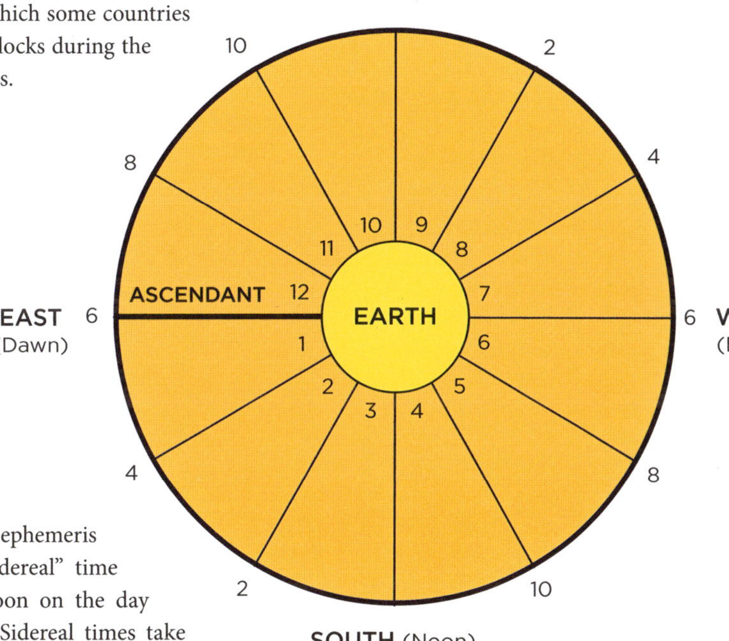

- Consult an ephemeris to find the "sidereal" time by GMT at noon on the day of your birth. Sidereal times take account of the fact that the Earth rotates on its axis in a fraction less than 24 hours. If you were born after noon, you need to add (or if before noon, subtract) a further allowance.

▲ The inner disk sits over the top of the outer disk and shows how the houses are divided.

THE HOUSES

Each of the 12 houses is connected with a specific area of the individual's life for prediction purposes.

♈ **First House:** Strongly concerned with the self, this house shows how the person presents his or her personality to the rest of the world. Also connected with childhood, with development, and with any new beginning. The ascending sign will always tend to dominate this house, though there is also a connection with Aries and the planet Mars. Any planet that transits this house is likely to set off some new trend in the person's life.

♉ **Second House:** This house is connected strongly with possessions, including money, goods, property, and even the prospects for earning or accumulating more money. Personal security is part of this, too. The person's capabilities (including artistic ones) are included. There are connections with Taurus and the planet Venus.

♊ **Third House:** The subjects concerning this house pertain to communications, the relationship of the individual to the nearby environment via letters, phone calls, and short journeys. Family members, neighbors, and acquaintances are frequently involved, though business relationships might also be included. Everyday contact with others is important. The sign connected with the third house is Gemini. Its planet is Mercury.

♋ **Fourth House:** The home environments and general domestic life are the subjects associated with the fourth house, though one's original home and roots may also be included. By extension, anything in this house may affect the property in which the subject lives, or the people with whom he or she lives, or even someone (like a mother) who was important during his or her formative years. The sign connected with the fourth house is Cancer. Its planet is Mars.

♌ **Fifth House:** This is considered the "fun" house. It is connected with leisure pursuits of any kind that can allow self-expression and bring happiness to the individual. These include hobbies, sports, the arts, holidays, and vacations. Lovemaking is also influenced by this house, as are pregnancy and children. (Here, "children" can also be taken to mean one's ideas, plans, and nurturing of nonliving creations.) The Sun and the zodiac sign of Leo are associated with the fifth house.

♍ **Sixth House:** This house concerns the subject's role in the community, and in particular the building of working relationships with superiors and subordinates. Service is the keyword in this instance, whether it is at work, in the house, or within some other realm of society. Another area covered by the sixth house is personal health (and/or illness). This includes doctors and hospitals, but also nutrition and wholesomeness. The sign connected with the sixth house is Virgo. Its planet is Mercury.

Seventh House: This house is the domain of important personal relationships, especially those with one's life partner, business partners, and any other relationships that require a good deal of cooperation on a regular basis. The focus here is on other people and there are indications as to which types the subject is best suited to (although enemies and competitors are also included). The zodiac sign connected with the seventh house is Libra. Its planet is Venus.

Eighth House: The emphasis with the eighth house is on being able to share things—particularly money and personal possessions. So any money matters that involve others (including wills, taxes, one's partners, income, and assets) are included here. So, too, are sexual relationships, shared feelings, and any kind of beginning or ending, such as birth or death. Great changes in outlook or lifestyle also fall within this scope. The zodiac sign connected with the eighth house is Scorpio and its planet may be Pluto or Mars.

Ninth House: The expansion of horizons is covered here, literally in terms of travel to distant places or communication with them, metaphorically through further education, and spiritually through religion or philosophy. Relationships with foreigners are included, though these may just be non-blood relatives. Whatever else, a mental expansion is generally involved. The sign is Sagittarius and the planet is Jupiter.

Tenth House: The subject's career, status, and goals are connected with the tenth house. The ego is at the center of it all, and how well any ambitions are achieved or frustrated—not just in one's career but also in, for example, political or creative pursuits. Authority figures and organizations are important here, as are one's relationships with and in them. The zodiac sign connected with this house is Capricorn. Its planet is Saturn.

Eleventh House: Friendships and group activities are central in the eleventh house, though more generally in the realm of hobbies and pastimes than at work. There can still be hopes and ambitions involved, but these are as much for the group as for oneself. All kinds of learning (though mostly for pleasure) are included. Some unconventional or eccentric activities could be involved. The zodiac sign connected with this house is Aquarius. Its planet may be Saturn or Uranus.

Twelfth House: This is the house concerned with solitariness—one's inner feelings, worries, psychological sufferings, and doubts. The twelfth house is full of negative influences, often prophesying ill health and weakness, although some positive influences, such as self-sacrifice, secret love, and hidden talent are also included. This is the place of illusions, daydreams, and exclusion from normal life. The zodiac sign connected with this house is Pisces. Its planet may be Neptune or Jupiter.

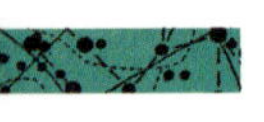

THE PLANETS

The seven "planets" of the ancients were the Sun, the Moon (neither of which is actually a planet, of course), Mercury, Venus, Mars, Jupiter, and Saturn, all of which were visible to the naked eye. The word planet comes from the Greek *planetes*, meaning "wanderer," because to the ancients they appeared to be wandering about against the fixed backcloth of stars.

Since the invention of the telescope, the other three planets of our Solar System, Uranus, Neptune, and Pluto (although this, too, has recently lost its planetary designation), have been discovered, although these are so distant and take so long to move through their orbits that their effect upon any astrological predictions is relatively small.

Each of the planets has certain characteristics attached to it, and these vary a little according to the zodiacal sign in which that planet was at the subject's birth or will be in the near future. These characteristics and the prospects associated with them will be modified again according to which of the houses that planet is in (or was in at the subject's birth, or is moving into during a future period that is being predicted). This kind of analysis is the very stuff of which detailed astrological prediction is made.

☉ **The Sun:** As the source of life and the "father" of the whole family of planets, the Sun has the most powerful influence upon an individual's personality. The Sun represents self-integration, authority, and vitality. It rules both the heart and the spine. As a powerful "masculine" force, it may be seen as governing the creative and generative power of man; for a woman the Sun represents power and career prospects, but also the important men in her life. The good side of the Sun's influence is effective leadership; the bad side of its influence is arrogance and intolerance.

☾ **The Moon:** With its overriding "female" qualities, the Moon represents the response to life—the moods and emotions. The Moon controls the qualities of intuition, affection, and spirituality. Because the Moon is associated with water—through its influence on the tides—it stands for changes, motions, and rhythms, including pregnancy and the physical changes of life. Each time the Moon is full or new it has an effect on one's fortunes, and the occasional eclipses (every few months) are also very significant. The Moon rules the stomach, breasts, ovaries, and digestive system. The negative features of the Moon are moodiness, impulsiveness, and a tendency toward excessive passivity.

The Moon and all the other planets are affected by their passage through the signs of the zodiac, as the Sun is, but this introductory guide will not list them all.

☿ **Mercury:** As the messenger of the gods in Roman mythology, it is no surprise to find that this planet's main astrological symbolism is communication. To be mercurial is to be bright, witty, volatile, and physically and mentally agile; and so it is with people born under Mercury.

SOLAR INFLUENCE

The Sun influences the signs of the zodiac as it passes through them. A person may display the following characteristics as this happens:

ARIES:	Enterprising, enjoying control; perhaps opinionated or confrontational.
TAURUS:	Persistent, resourceful; stubborn, a bad enemy.
GEMINI:	Versatile, communicative; can be vague or inconsistent.
CANCER:	Imaginative, shrewd, home-loving; may be shy or self-pitying.
LEO:	(The Sun's own sign) powerful, confident, dignified; or boastful, attention-seeking.
VIRGO:	Thoughtful, modest, efficient; may be fussy or interfering.
LIBRA:	Easygoing, diplomatic, and friendly; perhaps indecisive or lazy; may lack confidence.
SCORPIO:	Passionate, secretive, determined; may be jealous or brooding.
SAGITTARIUS:	Optimistic, enthusiastic, tolerant, loving freedom; or extravagant and restless.
CAPRICORN:	Practical, serious, hard-working; may be reserved, selfish.
AQUARIUS:	Independent, idealistic; perhaps rebellious, too unconventional.
PISCES:	Sympathetic, kind, emotional; but impractical, secretive, timid.

The head rules the heart where this planet is concerned. Mercury is associated with the nervous system, the brain, the lungs, and the thyroid. There is also an association with childhood and youth (this is because Mercury is the smallest of the planets), and with education. On the negative side of this planet's influences are tendencies toward impetuousness and irrational moods; Mercury is also something of a trickster.

Venus: This planet is concerned with harmony and unity. Venus stands for friendship and love, yet the connection with unbridled sexual passion is often overstated. The love of beauty, elegance, artistry, and peace are traits. The throat, kidneys, and parathyroid glands are Venus's concern. Negative qualities include tendencies toward weakness, shyness, and passivity in both men and women alike.

Mars: Mars represents an active, energetic, and healthy character, full of male passions. It is not necessarily warlike, despite tradition, although individuals may, perhaps, possess a quick temper. Other traits are fearlessness, tenacity, and straightforwardness. On the negative side, a person may be deemed too aggressive and shallow. The sex glands, urinary system, and kidneys are governed by Mars.

Jupiter: This, the largest of all the planets in the Solar System, symbolizes qualities such as expansion, improvement, cheerfulness, optimism, and a certain broad-mindedness. Attitudes are mature, generous, and big-hearted, though moral and conservative. Generally affable and unselfish, seeking success but not materialistic, Jupiter represents mature middle age. The negative side of this planet includes conceit, exaggeration, perhaps even criminal activity. It controls the body's healing, the liver, and pituitary gland.

Saturn: Personified as an old man, Saturn's greatest strengths are responsibility and capability. The virtues of the Saturnian include caution, control, patience, and thrift. This is an unhappy planet, however, bringing difficult circumstances, and, on its own, would be a bad influence in anybody's horoscope. There is a lack of humor, of happiness, or of any real emotion. The body's skin, bones, and teeth are ruled by Saturn.

Uranus: Representing change, freedom, and originality, Uranus has an uncertain effect upon horoscopes. Despite its great distance from Earth, it spends seven years in each sign, and therefore it is a little more influential than might be supposed. There is a certain mysticism and willingness to behave out of character associated with Uranus subjects. Uranus controls the circulatory system and the pineal gland.

Neptune: Even less significant than Uranus, due to its greater distance and slower pace, Neptune is the mystic planet, standing for intuition and the imagination. Subjects possess great sensitivity, although they tend toward vagueness, chaos, and self-destroying addictions. Neptune rules the spine, parts of the nervous system, and the thalamus. It has been in only some of the constellations this century.

Pluto: The planet of the unknown and the unconscious, Pluto stands for transformation. Its subjects are individualists. Its effects need to be faced alone. Pluto controls the reproductive system, and it is associated with beginnings and endings (birth and death). Only a few signs this century have been affected by it.

◀ A diagram of the planets as featured in the **Breviary of Love**, a 13th-century Provençal codex by Ermengol de Béziers.

CHINESE ASTROLOGY

The Chinese astrological system of animal years has achieved such a high profile during the last few years, with many books published on the subject and features appearing in major magazines on the occasion of each Chinese New Year, that there can be few people still unaware of it.

Chinese astrology features 12 animal year signs that follow each other in a regular cycle. For example, 2005 was the year of the Rooster, so was 1993, and before that, 1981. The next year of the Rooster will be 2017.

The 12 animals in the cycle are (in order): the Rat, the Buffalo or Ox, the Tiger, the Rabbit or Hare, the Dragon, the Snake, the Horse, the Goat, the Monkey, the Rooster or Cockerel, the Dog, and the Pig or Boar. It is important to realize that there is absolutely no connection between Chinese astrology and Western astrology. No correlation exists between the 12 Chinese animals and the 12 signs of the Western zodiac.

The basis of the Chinese animal system is that people born in a particular year are likely to possess a set of given personality characteristics. So a person born in 1960 (the year of the Rat) will be different from a person born in 1959 (the year of the Pig) or 1961 (the year of the Buffalo), but will tend to have some similarities with a person born in 1948 or 1972 (also years of the Rat). This is greatly simplifying the Chinese system; in fact, there are subtle differences between people born in different years carrying the same sign.

▲ This 17th-century wall painting from a temple in northern China depicts the astrological sign of the Tiger.

THE RAT

Rats are often opportunists, with charm and tenacity. They are ambitious, often greedy. You will find them in company (for they tend not to be loners) but you may also find them arriving late, as punctuality is not one of their strengths. Rats dislike performing routine work and are often to be found in jobs or professions where each day brings something new.

- In love, the Rat is most compatible with other Rats and very compatible with Buffaloes, Dragons, or Monkeys, but they do not get along well at all with Goats or Roosters.
- In marriage, the Rat should go for a Dragon, or perhaps a Goat or Pig, but certainly not a Tiger, Cat, or Horse.
- In business, the spouse could also be the ideal business partner, for here, too, the Dragon is the best bet.

Famous Rats:
Shakespeare, Wolfgang Amadeus Mozart, President George H. W. Bush, Joan Collins, Prince Charles, and Cameron Diaz were all born in the Year of the Rat.

RAT YEARS

Date ranges for the Year of the Rat during the last 100 years

FEBRUARY 18, 1912	.... to	FEBRUARY 5, 1913
FEBRUARY 5, 1924	.... to	JANUARY 23, 1925
JANUARY 24, 1936	.... to	FEBRUARY 10, 1937
FEBRUARY 10, 1948	.... to	JANUARY 28, 1949
JANUARY 28, 1960	.... to	FEBRUARY 14, 1961
FEBRUARY 15, 1972	.... to	FEBRUARY 2, 1973
FEBRUARY 2, 1984	.... to	FEBRUARY 19, 1985
FEBRUARY 09, 1996	.... to	FEBRUARY 6, 1997
FEBRUARY 7, 2008	.... to	JANUARY 25, 2009

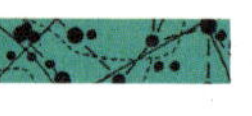

THE BUFFALO

Buffaloes are hard-working, strong-minded, and extremely punctual. They tend not to have close friends and often suffer problems in love and marriage. Continuity is important to them, and they dislike change or interruptions. You will find Buffaloes in routine jobs everywhere, in which they are often highly valued.

- In love, the Buffalo will relate well with a Rooster or a Pig, but should not attempt a personal relationship with either a Tiger or a Goat.
- In marriage, only a Rooster is really compatible, since Buffaloes are often very difficult to live with; other Buffaloes, Tigers, Dragons, Horses, and Dogs are best avoided.
- In business, the Buffalo gets along best with a Horse or a Pig, but not at all with a Tiger, Dragon, Snake, Goat, Monkey, or Dog.

Famous Buffaloes:
Margaret Thatcher, Robert Redford, Princess Diana, Marlene Dietrich, and Fidel Castro.

BUFFALO YEARS

Date ranges for the Year of the Buffalo during the last 100 years

FEBRUARY 6, 1913	.... to	JANUARY 25, 1914
JANUARY 24, 1925	.... to	FEBRUARY 12, 1926
FEBRUARY 11, 1937	.... to	JANUARY 30, 1938
JANUARY 29, 1949	.... to	FEBRUARY 16, 1950
FEBRUARY 15, 1961	.... to	FEBRUARY 4, 1962
FEBRUARY 3, 1973	.... to	JANUARY 22, 1974
FEBRUARY 20, 1985	.... to	FEBRUARY 8, 1986
FEBRUARY 7, 1997	.... to	JANUARY 27, 1998
JANUARY 26, 2009	.... to	FEBRUARY 14, 2010

TIGER YEARS

Date ranges for the Year of the Tiger during the last 100 years

JANUARY 26, 1914	.... to	FEBRUARY 13, 1915
FEBRUARY 13, 1926	.... to	FEBRUARY 1, 1927
JANUARY 31, 1938	.... to	FEBRUARY 18, 1939
FEBRUARY 17, 1950	.... to	FEBRUARY 5, 1951
FEBRUARY 5, 1962	.... to	JANUARY 24, 1963
JANUARY 23, 1974	.... to	FEBRUARY 10, 1975
FEBRUARY 9, 1986	.... to	JANUARY 28, 1987
JANUARY 28, 1998	.... to	FEBRUARY 15, 1999
FEBRUARY 14, 2010	.... to	FEBRUARY 2, 2011

THE TIGER

Tigers are dynamic, "ideas" people, liable to become impatient, to quarrel, to complain loudly, and to be noticed wherever they are. They can be elegant and flamboyant. Their lives are often unpredictable, with violent ups and downs. They lack endurance and often make changes just for the sake of it.

- In love, the Tiger has greatest compatibility with the Dragon and only slightly less with the Horse; Buffaloes, Snakes, and other Tigers are worth a Tiger's while avoiding.
- In marriage, a Dog is the best partner, or perhaps a Dragon or a Pig; but a Tiger should not marry a Rat, Buffalo, or Snake.
- In business, the Tiger will do very well with either Dragons or Horses and should not get mixed up with Buffaloes, other Tigers, Snakes, Roosters, or Dogs.

Famous Tigers:
Marilyn Monroe was an archetypal Tiger. Others are Sir Alec Guinness and Queen Elizabeth II.

THE RABBIT

Rabbits are sensitive and good listeners. Push them hard and you should get what you want. They like a quiet life (especially at home) and try to avoid strong emotions of any kind. A Rabbit is likely to be methodical in all things, light-hearted, and not very deep thinkers. Rabbits are good to have around—they are often very popular.

- In marriage, the Rabbit is easy to please, and an ideal partner for a Dragon, a Snake, a Horse, or another Rabbit; only a Rat or a Rooster should be avoided.

- In business, the Rabbit is best with another Rabbit, highly compatible with a Rat, Dragon, Snake, Goat, or Pig, and only in trouble when dealing with a Tiger or a Monkey.

- In love, the Rabbit gets along perfectly with a Dragon, very well with a Horse, a Goat, or another Rabbit, and fairly well with a Buffalo, a Snake, a Monkey, a Dog, and a Pig; only the Rooster is incompatible.

Famous Rabbits:
Bob Hope, Jodie Foster, David Frost, and Queen Victoria.

RABBIT YEARS

Date ranges for the Year of the Rabbit during the last 100 years

FEBRUARY 14, 1915	.... to	FEBRUARY 2, 1916
FEBRUARY 2,1927	.... to	JANUARY 22, 1928
FEBRUARY 19, 1939	.... to	FEBRUARY 7, 1940
FEBRUARY 6, 1951	.... to	FEBRUARY 26, 1952
JANUARY 25, 1963	.... to	FEBRUARY 12, 1964
FEBRUARY 11,1975	.... to	JANUARY 30, 1976
JANUARY 29, 1987	.... to	FEBRUARY 16, 1988
FEBRUARY 16, 1999	.... to	FEBRUARY 4, 2000
FEBRUARY 3, 2011	.... to	JANUARY 22, 2012

DRAGON YEARS

Date ranges for the Year of the Dragon during the last 100 years

FEBRUARY 3, 1916	.... to	JANUARY 22, 1917
JANUARY 23, 1928	.... to	FEBRUARY 9, 1929
FEBRUARY 8, 1940	.... to	JANUARY 26, 1941
FEBRUARY 27, 1952	.... to	FEBRUARY 13, 1953
FEBRUARY 13, 1964	.... to	FEBRUARY 1, 1965
JANUARY 31, 1976	.... to	FEBRUARY 17, 1977
FEBRUARY 17, 1988	.... to	FEBRUARY 5, 1989
FEBRUARY 5, 2000	.... to	JANUARY 23, 2001
JANUARY 23, 2012	.... to	FEBRUARY 9, 2013

THE DRAGON

A Dragon tends to be somewhat flashy and arrogant, but also tends to be both admired and hated, with good friends and bad enemies. Unlike Buffaloes they hate routine. Dragons are mostly monogamous and loyal (although they need a good partner to look after them). They are often generous and almost invariably awkward.

- In business, Dragons do well with Rats, Tigers, Monkeys, Roosters, or Pigs, but should beware of Buffaloes and Dogs.

- In marriage, Dragons can have great relationships with Rats, Monkeys, or Roosters and pretty good ones with Tigers, Rabbits, and Snakes; but Dragons must avoid other Dragons, Dogs, and Buffaloes.

- In love, the dragon is superbly compatible with Tigers, Cats, Snakes, Horses, and Monkeys and extremely good with Rats or Goats; only with Dogs or other Dragons are there likely to be problems.

Famous Dragons:
Shirley Temple, Cliff Richard, Martin Sheen, and Nicholas Cage were all born in the Year of the Dragon.

THE SNAKE

Snakes are wise and tenacious people, not necessarily beautiful but most often attractive. They tend toward infidelity but are also paradoxically very possessive. An artistic talent is a strong possibility, as is the ability to make money. Although preferring idleness and being prone to making wrong decisions, Snakes are good companions by virtue of their sense of humor, unwillingness to quarrel, and ability to adapt to circumstances.

- In business, no relationships are perfectly smooth. Snakes do best on their own, but can manage with Rabbits.

- In marriage, the Snake has plenty of choice, though a Rabbit is best, while a Tiger is impossible.

- In love, the Snake is perfect for a Dragon, pretty good with a Horse, and only incompatible with a Tiger or another Snake.

Famous Snakes:
Presidents Abraham Lincoln and John F. Kennedy, Bob Dylan, Muhammad Ali, and Placido Domingo were all born in the Year of the Snake.

SNAKE YEARS

Date ranges for the Year of the Snake during the last 100 years

JANUARY 23, 1917	.... to	FEBRUARY 10, 1918
FEBRUARY 10, 1929	.... to	JANUARY 29, 1930
JANUARY 27, 1941	.... to	FEBRUARY 14, 1942
FEBRUARY 14, 1953	.... to	FEBRUARY 2, 1954
FEBRUARY 2, 1965	.... to	JANUARY 20, 1966
FEBRUARY 18, 1977	.... to	FEBRUARY 6,1978
FEBRUARY 6, 1989	.... to	JANUARY 26, 1990
JANUARY 24, 2001	.... to	FEBRUARY 11, 2002
FEBRUARY 10, 2013	.... to	JANUARY 30, 2014

HORSE YEARS

Date ranges for the Year of the Horse during the last 100 years

FEBRUARY 11, 1918	.... to	JANUARY 31, 1919
JANUARY 30, 1930	.... to	FEBRUARY 16, 1931
FEBRUARY 15, 1942	.... to	FEBRUARY 4, 1943
FEBRUARY 3, 1954	.... to	JANUARY 23, 1955
JANUARY 21, 1966	.... to	FEBRUARY 4, 1967
FEBRUARY 7, 1978	.... to	JANUARY 27, 1979
JANUARY 27, 1990	.... to	FEBRUARY 14, 1991
FEBRUARY 12, 2002	.... to	JANUARY 31, 2003
JANUARY 31, 2014	.... to	FEBRUARY 18, 2014

THE HORSE

Horses are elegant, easygoing, and with a good sense of humor. They may possess great sex appeal. Not that the social side is all they care about—they are often hard workers, good decision makers, and natural leaders. They love company and are excellent listeners. Their only weaknesses are falling in love too easily and making changes too frequently.

- In love, they are superbly compatible with Goats, Dogs, and other Horses, pretty good with Tigers, Rabbits, and Snakes, but should avoid Monkeys, Roosters, and Pigs.

- In marriage, their choice is wide, with the Rabbit, Goat, and other Horses being best, a Rooster or Dog very good, but never a Rat, Buffalo, or Monkey.

- In business, a Horse should choose a Tiger or a Rooster as a business partner, though good results can also be expected with a Buffalo, Rabbit, Dragon, or Goat, but not so with a Rat, a Pig, or another Horse.

Famous Horses:
Clint Eastwood, Barbara Streisand, and Emma Watson are famous Horses.

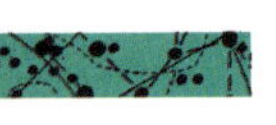

THE GOAT

A Goat enjoys life, but in his or her own way and preferably without restraints of any kind. Goats are artistic and sociable. They also tend to be popular. However, Goats can also be fickle, insecure, and bad at making decisions. Not normally leaders, Goats are quite easily—sometimes happily—led or influenced by others.

- In love, the Goat has little control and will get along very well with a Horse or perhaps a Rabbit or a Dragon; but will not get along so well with a Rat, Buffalo, Rooster, or Pig.
- In marriage, the Horse is again best, and a Rabbit, Dragon, or Pig can be quite compatible; Roosters and Dogs should be avoided.
- In business, a Goat can get along quite well with a Rabbit, a Horse, or a Pig, but will not get along at all with a Buffalo, a Rooster, or a Dog.

Famous Goats:
Mikhail Gorbachev, Andy Warhol, John Major, Mick Jagger, and Michelangelo were all born in the Year of the Goat.

GOAT YEARS

Date ranges for the Year of the Goat during the last 100 years

FEBRUARY 1, 1919	.... to	FEBRUARY 19, 1920
FEBRUARY 17, 1931	.... to	FEBRUARY 5, 1932
FEBRUARY 5, 1943	.... to	JANUARY 24, 1944
JANUARY 24, 1955	.... to	FEBRUARY 11, 1956
FEBRUARY 9, 1967	.... to	JANUARY 29, 1968
JANUARY 28, 1979	.... to	FEBRUARY 15, 1980
FEBRUARY 15, 1991	.... to	FEBRUARY 3, 1992
FEBRUARY 1, 2003	.... to	JANUARY 21, 2004
FEBRUARY 19, 2015	.... to	FEBRUARY 7, 2016

MONKEY YEARS

Date ranges for the Year of the Monkey during the last 100 years

FEBRUARY 2, 1908	.... to	JANUARY 21, 1909
FEBRUARY 20, 1920	.... to	FEBRUARY 7, 1921
FEBRUARY 6, 1932	.... to	JANUARY 25, 1933
JANUARY 25, 1944	.... to	FEBRUARY 12, 1945
FEBRUARY 12, 1956	.... to	JANUARY 30, 1957
JANUARY 30, 1968	.... to	FEBRUARY 16, 1969
FEBRUARY 16, 1980	.... to	FEBRUARY 4, 1981
FEBRUARY 4, 1992	.... to	JANUARY 22, 1993
JANUARY 22, 2004	.... to	FEBRUARY 8, 2005

THE MONKEY

The Monkey is a tricky person, quick, opportunistic, and often good with numbers. He or she knows it, too, and is not modest. Monkeys have excellent memories and possess the potential to be very successful. Not succeeding would be due to impatience, superficiality, and inability to share. At the same time, Monkeys can be generous and thoughtful people.

- In love, the Monkey is highly compatible with Dragons, Pigs, and other Monkeys, compatible with Rats, and completely at odds with both Horses and Dogs.
- In marriage, it is very similar, with Dragons, Pigs, and other Monkeys making ideal mates, Goats making good ones, and Horses or Roosters tending to be the worst.
- In business, the Monkey can work well in partnership with a Dragon or a Pig and not at all with a Buffalo, Rabbit, Rooster, or Dog.

Famous Monkeys:
Michael Douglas, Elizabeth Taylor, Sebastian Coe, Ian Fleming, and Diana Ross were born in the Year of the Monkey.

THE ROOSTER

An honest and generous person, the Rooster likes to offer you plenty of free advice whether you have asked for it or not (although some Roosters do prove to be less extrovert). They can be both miserly or rash spenders, depending on their nature. Almost always, however, Roosters are efficient, methodical people, though perhaps lacking in initiative at times.

- In marriage, the Dragon is ideal, the Buffalo, Snake, or Horse almost as good, while the Rabbit, Goat, Monkey, or another Rooster are impossible.

- In business, the Rooster gets along well with Dragons and Horses, slightly with Buffaloes, but hardly at all with any other animal types.

- In love, only the Buffalo is compatible, since Roosters are really interested in more permanent relationships.

Famous Roosters:
Eric Clapton, Errol Flynn, Beyoncé Knowles, Renee Zellweger, Jennifer Aniston, and Jennifer Lopez were all born in the Year of the Rooster.

ROOSTER YEARS

Date ranges for the Year of the Rooster during the last 100 years

JANUARY 22, 1909	.... to	FEBRUARY 9, 1910
FEBRUARY 8, 1921	.... to	JANUARY 27, 1922
JANUARY 26, 1933	.... to	FEBRUARY 13, 1934
FEBRUARY 13, 1945	.... to	FEBRUARY 1, 1946
JANUARY 31, 1957	.... to	FEBRUARY 17, 1958
FEBRUARY 17, 1969	.... to	FEBRUARY 5, 1970
FEBRUARY 5, 1981	.... to	JANUARY 24, 1982
JANUARY 23, 1993	.... to	FEBRUARY 9, 1994
FEBRUARY 9, 2005	.... to	JANUARY 28, 2006

DOG YEARS

Date ranges for the Year of the Dog during the last 100 years

FEBRUARY 10, 1910	.... to	JANUARY 29, 1911
JANUARY 28, 1922	.... to	FEBRUARY 15, 1923
FEBRUARY 14,1934	.... to	FEBRUARY 3, 1935
FEBRUARY 2, 1946	.... to	JANUARY 21, 1947
FEBRUARY 18, 1958	.... to	FEBRUARY 7, 1959
FEBRUARY 6, 1970	.... to	JANUARY 26, 1971
JANUARY 25, 1982	.... to	FEBRUARY 12, 1983
FEBRUARY 10, 1994	.... to	JANUARY 30, 1995
JANUARY 29, 2006	.... to	FEBRUARY 17, 2007

THE DOG

Dogs are always very hard-working people. They also make genuine and loyal friends and can be great opponents of injustice. They may be stubborn in nature or get bogged down with small details, and they generally do best as followers, not leaders. They have very high standards by which they judge themselves and those around them. They can be pessimistic.

- In love, the Dog is wonderfully suited to a Horse or a Pig and not at all compatible with a Dragon or a Goat.
- In marriage, a Tiger or a Pig is ideal, while a Buffalo, a Dragon, or a Goat is best avoided.
- In business, only the Pig will make a good partner for the Dog; most other animal partnerships will not succeed in the work environment.

Famous Dogs:
President George W. Bush, Madonna, Liza Minnelli, Winston Churchill, Michael Jackson, and Kevin Bacon were all born in the Year of the Dog.

THE PIG

Pigs are always very hard workers and can be great moneymakers, especially when working as part of a team. They are open, straightforward people, often strong-minded and self-confident without being overly cocky. Their generosity and steadfastness make them excellent friends. Pigs can fall in love easily and tend to take rejection very badly.

- In love, the Pig is pretty compatible with all other animal signs, except the Horse, though Pigs are especially suited to a Dog or another Pig.
- In marriage, things are even better for the Pig: Ideal partners are Monkeys, Dogs, or other Pigs; however, no signs are ruled out completely.
- When it comes to the business world, the Pig works best alongside a Monkey or a Dragon. Pigs should avoid Horses at all costs.

Famous Pigs:
President Ronald Reagan, Woody Allen, Elton John, Kevin Spacey, and Winona Ryder were all born in the Year of the Pig.

PIG YEARS

Date ranges for the Year of the Pig during the last 100 years

JANUARY 30, 1911	.... to	FEBRUARY 17, 1912
FEBRUARY 16, 1923	.... to	FEBRUARY 4, 1924
FEBRUARY 4, 1935	.... to	JANUARY 23, 1936
JANUARY 22, 1947	.... to	FEBRUARY 9, 1948
FEBRUARY 8, 1959	.... to	JANUARY 27, 1960
JANUARY 27, 1971	.... to	FEBRUARY 14, 1972
FEBRUARY 13, 1983	.... to	FEBRUARY 1, 1984
JANUARY 31, 1995	.... to	FEBRUARY 18, 1996
FEBRUARY 18, 2007	.... to	FEBRUARY 6, 2008

ASTROLOGY TODAY

Fortune-telling has an extremely long history—longer than any written records show. Hundreds of methods have been used and discarded over the centuries. Astrology is just one of them.

The Eastern mind has always been more open to astrology than the Western mind, and despite the rise of modern science and technology, mystical ways of interpreting the world are regarded as equally important. In the West in recent years, astrology has witnessed a resurgence, perhaps as people decided that neither science nor religion has all the answers to life's deepest questions.

In the second half of this book, you will learn more about the Western zodiac and how your date of birth influences your personality traits and drives a large number of the important decisions that you make during the course of your life.

▼ A horoscope wheel, complete with planetary markings.

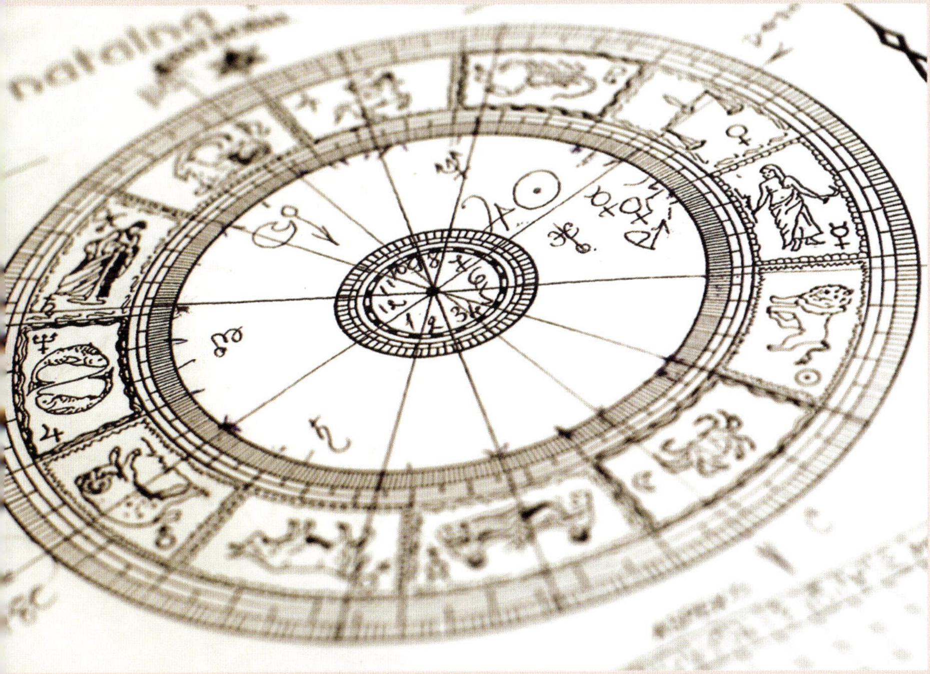

Coma Berenices
Leo
Cancer
Hydra
Canis min.
Auriga
Via lactea
Orion

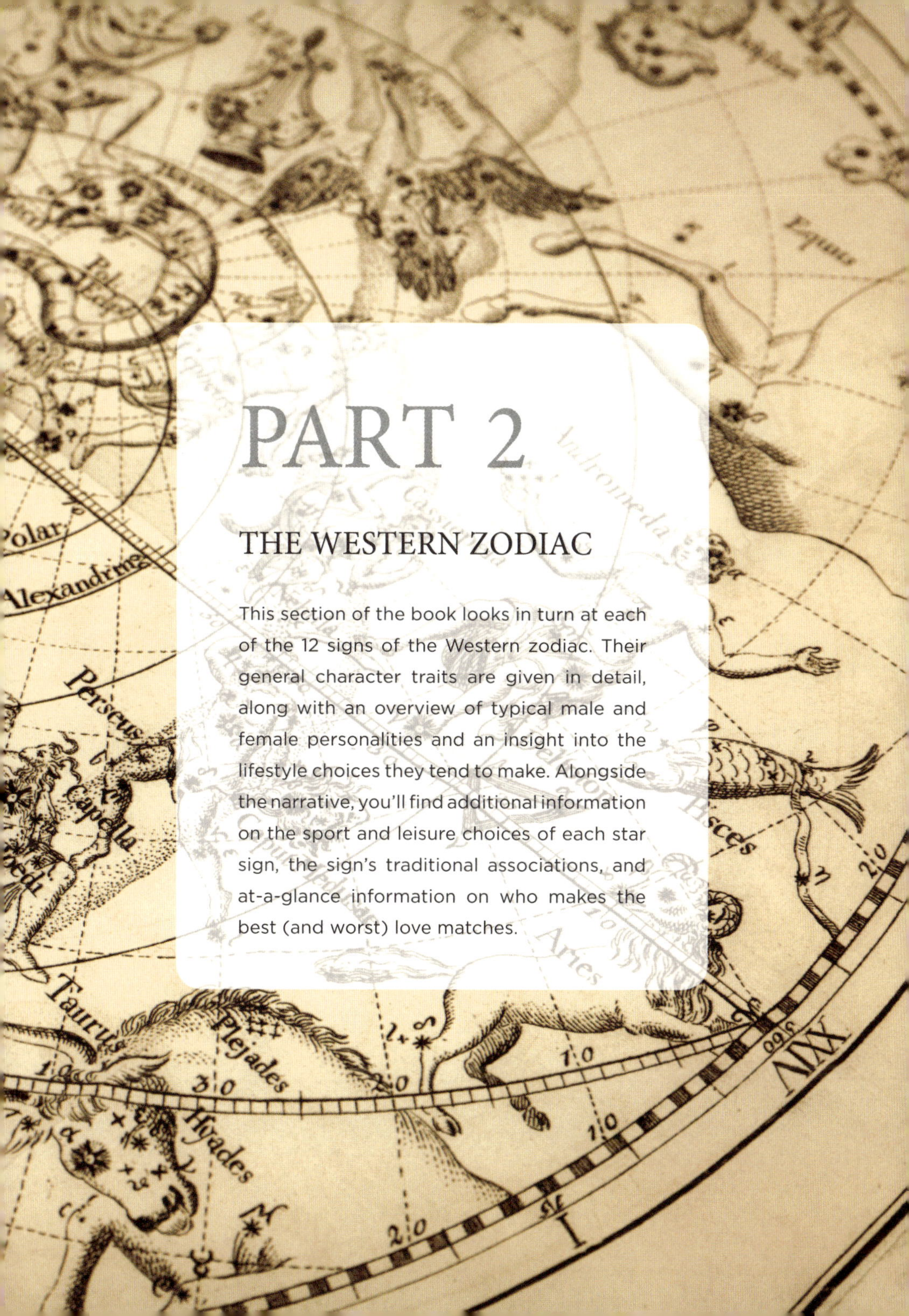

PART 2

THE WESTERN ZODIAC

This section of the book looks in turn at each of the 12 signs of the Western zodiac. Their general character traits are given in detail, along with an overview of typical male and female personalities and an insight into the lifestyle choices they tend to make. Alongside the narrative, you'll find additional information on the sport and leisure choices of each star sign, the sign's traditional associations, and at-a-glance information on who makes the best (and worst) love matches.

SIGNS OF THE ZODIAC

There are various ways of classifying the 12 signs of the Western Zodiac, and these help us to understand the fundamental nature of each one—the things they have in common and how they differ.

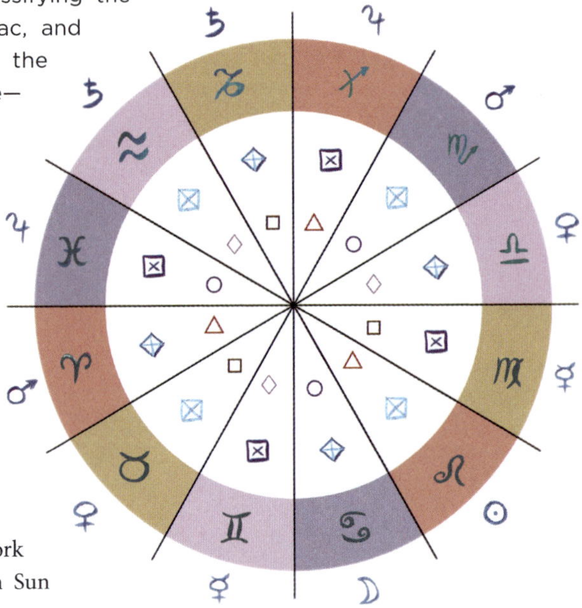

Each of the 12 zodiac signs belongs to both an element and mode group. By studying these, we can learn, for example, that Aries is a Cardinal Fire sign, combining the elemental qualities of enthusiasm and assertion with the "mode" qualities of initiation and action. You can easily work out the combination for your own Sun sign and those of family and friends.

▲ An astrological chart detailing the zodiac signs, their rulers, and their elemental properties.

THE ELEMENTS

The 12 signs are divided into four elements: Fire, Air, Water, and Earth. Each element has three signs within its group, and because of this, they are also named the "triplicities," meaning groups of three.

Fire and Air are known as the positive or masculine elements, representing energy rising upward and extroversion. The Fire signs are Aries, Leo, and Sagittarius. Fire signs are enthusiastic, self-confident, assertive, courageous, and usually display a great love of life. The Air signs are Gemini, Libra, and Aquarius. Air is spacious and free moving, symbolizing thought and intellect. These signs love thinking, and can be quite analytical and detached, but they also need to be able to communicate effectively.

The feminine and negative elements are Water and Earth. They tend toward introversion, and represent energy moving downward. The Earth signs are Taurus, Virgo, and Capricorn. These signs are very down-to-earth, solid, practical, and concerned with the material world. The three Water signs are Cancer, Scorpio,

ELEMENTS AND THE ZODIAC

Sign	Symbol	Element	Mode	Type
ARIES	♈	Fire	Cardinal	Masculine
TAURUS	♉	Earth	Fixed	Feminine
GEMINI	♊	Air	Mutable	Masculine
CANCER	♋	Water	Cardinal	Feminine
LEO	♌	Fire	Fixed	Masculine
VIRGO	♍	Earth	Mutable	Feminine
LIBRA	♎	Air	Cardinal	Masculine
SCORPIO	♏	Water	Fixed	Feminine
SAGITTARIUS	♐	Fire	Mutable	Masculine
CAPRICORN	♑	Earth	Cardinal	Feminine
AQUARIUS	♒	Air	Fixed	Masculine
PISCES	♓	Water	Mutable	Feminine

and Pisces. Water signs are in tune with their emotions, and usually have powerful imaginations and feelings.

A strong affinity exists between signs of each element group because they share many of the same characteristics. The six positive signs will have much in common, as will the six negative.

THE MODES

Another way to classify the signs is by their modes. The modes describe how a sign takes action and its phase of manifestation. There are three modes, each with four signs. These groupings are also termed the "quadruplicities." The first mode is named "Cardinal," or fundamental, and this group consists of Aries, Cancer, Libra, and Capricorn. Cardinal signs are good at initiating and taking action. They represent the four seasonal equinox points, with Aries beginning on March 21, Cancer on June 21, and so on.

The second mode is "Fixed." The Fixed signs are Taurus, Leo, Scorpio, and Aquarius. Fixed signs are drawn toward keeping things stable and enduring. When the Sun is in the Fixed signs, each season comes to its peak.

The last mode is "Mutable," which means changeable and adaptable. The Mutable signs are Gemini, Virgo, Sagittarius, and Pisces. These four signs are highly adaptable and quick to change or move on. They are found at the end of each season, when nature is in transition.

▲ Detail of Tycho Brahe from the celestial atlas **Harmonia Macrocosmica**, by Andreas Cellarius in 1660–61.

THE SUN AND THE MOON

Each sign is associated with one or two planets in particular, that are then said to rule the sign. These rulerships show similarities between certain planets and signs, and help astrologers to understand the meaning of both.

The Sun shows your basic spirit and vitality, your type of power, and how you grow as an individual. Much of your creative drive is symbolized by your Sun sign, and the Sun is always one of the most important factors in any chart, representing your fundamental consciousness and how you express your will. The Sun in a woman's chart is one of the indications of what sort of man she will be attracted to. The Sun rules the sign of Leo.

The Moon represents your instincts and basic emotional responses, giving information about your subconscious and unconscious mind, and how you react defensively. In a somewhat overly male-dominated modern world, the Moon is a vital indicator of the feminine side of your nature and is linked to childbirth. It also represents what sort of environment you feel comfortable in, and for a man, the Moon often reveals the type of woman he is drawn toward. The Moon rules the sign of Cancer.

THE PLANETS

Mercury reveals how you think and communicate—how your mind works, what you think about, and your ability to make decisions. It can symbolize intelligence. Mercury is a planet that is never more than one sign away from the Sun. This means that your Mercury will be placed either in the same sign as your Sun, or the one preceeding or following it. Thus, if your sign is Cancer, your Mercury sign will be either Gemini, Cancer, or Leo. Therefore, the position of Mercury can strongly modify the influence of your Sun sign. For example, an Aries with Mercury in sensitive Pisces will be much more reflective and emotional than a typical Arien. Mercury rules Gemini and Virgo.

Venus represents how you relate to others and your image of love. It describes your behavior in relationships, as well as your social values and attitudes. It is also one of the planets that relates to finances. The placement of Venus in a man's chart depicts his image of an ideal mate. Venus rules the signs of Taurus and Libra.

Mars symbolizes your sexuality and energy. It also shows how you take action and initiate the impulsive desires you may have, and the ambitions arising from these. Mars represents your fighting spirit, or how you stand up for yourself. For a woman, the placement of Mars in her chart describes her image of an ideal man. Mars rules Aries, and also shares rulership of Scorpio with Pluto.

Jupiter represents your sense of opportunity. It shows your good fortune and luck in life, and how you are enabled to be positive. A strongly placed Jupiter can help you find much joy, happiness, and optimism. Jupiter rules Sagittarius, and shares rulership of Pisces with Neptune.

Saturn displays your level of discipline, and how you deal with restriction and delays. It concerns authority, hard work, and the handling of responsibility, and has therefore been called "the taskmaster." Saturn has sole rulership of Capricorn, and is a joint ruler with Uranus of Aquarius. In olden days, Saturn signified the extent of the known Solar System and because of this became linked with limitation but also with qualities of persistence and tenacity.

Since the outer three planets move very slowly through the heavens, they reveal generational themes as well as individual characteristics. For example, the generation of people born around the 1960s (all those born between September 1957 and September 1971), when Pluto was in the sign of Virgo, would share a concern for ecology and the environment suggested by this astrological placement.

▲ A plate showing the planisphere of Copernicus, from **Harmonia Macrocosmica** by Andreas Cellarius.

Uranus represents your urge for freedom and individuality. It can also show how you rebel against authority and why. Uranus is often featured in science fiction and the exploration of space. It is usually associated with originality, independence, and occasionally with rebellion.

Neptune is concerned with your sense of yearning, ideals, and desire to merge with something greater than yourself. It reveals how you seek to escape from the trials and tribulations of life.

Finally, Pluto signifies how you regenerate and transform yourself. It also covers taboos and that which is deeply hidden, such as buried feelings and emotions.

ARIES MARCH 21–APRIL 19

You are a natural leader. Born at the beginning of the zodiac, you are used to being first and possess a pioneering, determined spirit. Your abundant physical and mental energy helps you to make your mark on the world. For some Ariens this may be through sport; for others, work provides the necessary challenges—but whatever the field, all Ariens need outside activities in which to assert themselves, and seek action, daring, and adventure. You are at heart fearless, and this openness to meet life head-on is one of your greatest assets.

However, it can also be your undoing, as you have a tendency to rush in where angels fear to tread. Impulsive and gutsy, your initial reactions and decisions usually turn out well, but with age comes the wisdom that allows you to hold back when necessary.

As the infant of the zodiac, you are concerned with yourself, and sometimes selfishly ignore the feelings of others, although those around you do admire the sheer energy and enthusiasm you show in whatever it is you are doing.

Most Ariens are driven by a need to win, and this gives you a very competitive

▲ Aries is associated with The Emperor in tarot, which represents leadership, wealth, strength, intelligence, dominating emotion, and power over others.

▶ A detail showing the head of Aries, the Ram, from a 15th-century Persian translation of Al-Sufi's **The Book of Fixed Stars**, originally dated CE 964.

TRADITIONAL ASSOCIATIONS

Ariens are most closely associated with the following:

COLORS:	Red, white mixed with red
COUNTRIES:	Poland, Germany, England
TAROT CARD:	Number 4, The Emperor
FLOWERS:	Tiger lily
BIRTHSTONE:	Ruby, diamond
ANIMALS:	Ram, tiger, dragon
OCCUPATIONS:	Firefighter, police officer, psychiatrist, business executive
HERBS:	Nettles
TREES:	Thorn, chestnut, holly
CITIES:	Kraków, Florence, Brunswick, Naples
FOOD:	Garlic, onions, leeks, spicy foods

attitude. You simply must come first, and want to make sure that everyone else knows it. Because of this, you thrive on rivalry, which is fine as long as you can sometimes accept second place. You are not Superman, after all—even though you may try to be!

Always hungry for new experiences, you frequently rely on your great sense of humor to get the most out of life. Unfortunately for you, however, you tend to become bored and restless quite easily. Perseverance is one trait that most Ariens have to work on—it's all very well having an abundance of brilliant ideas, but without focus and discipline, it is very easy for nothing actually to happen. Once you find out what you really want to do in life, nothing can stop you from achieving your goals, and with considerable success.

THE ARIEN MAN

In appearance, the males of the sign are tall and lean, with a good bone structure and strong physical presence. You are energetic and walk with a quick, confident gait, taking long strides as you move. You may have a scar or mark on your head, often from a previous fight or adventure. You are a very physical person; that will almost certainly manifest itself in some sort of sporting activity. Because you are so in touch with your body and enjoy it, you fear physical disability more than most people.

Straightforward and direct, you throw yourself into life without thinking too much about the consequences. You enjoy taking the initiative, and won't be too happy having to follow others for long periods of time. You love simplicity and try to set clear goals, even on a day-to-day basis. The past does not hold back a typical Arien; however many times life knocks you down, you are able to pick yourself up and try again as your confidence is virtually inexhaustible, and so is your desire to prove yourself and get what you want.

Although independent and very much a "man's man" you gain tremendously from being in a loving relationship, as your blunt nature benefits from a woman's sensitivity.

▲ The vibrant colors of the tiger lily are said to represent wealth, affluence, and a sense of pride.

THE ARIEN WOMAN

Most Arien women are slim, as your active lifestyle doesn't allow you any time to get fat! Your body is usually lithe, and gives an impression of tremendous vitality. Like Arien males, you walk at a fast pace—often one or two steps ahead of your friends. You are a bit of a tomboy, and this will be reflected in the way that you dress.

You have a very talkative nature and, unlike many, are not afraid to assert yourself. This forthright manner can get you into trouble, and you are sometimes taken aback by the reactions you get.

▲ Rubies are said to represent vigor, enthusiasm, and a passion for life.

You are very idealistic, and will stick up for the underdog. If you are committed to a cause, you are prepared to fight with every ounce of your strength. You are one of life's optimists, and believe that you can achieve the impossible. Although you are undeniably feminine, you relate well to men, and often prefer their company. You are very independent, and are quite happy to live on your own. Arien women have a reputation for being emotionally tough, but secretly you desire a man who is strong enough to share your dreams.

DRESS SENSE

For most Ariens, one of the most important considerations when choosing the right clothes to wear is comfort. Yours is such a physical sign that you tend to avoid garments that restrict movement; even for work, comfort is always a must. Ariens love simplicity, and once you have found combinations that work well, tend to stick to them. Although you favor fairly conventional styles, if you want to wear something you will, regardless of what anyone else thinks. When it comes to selecting casual attire, sports clothes are a popular choice for both sexes. You love to feel physically free. In the meantime, for work clothes, you are attracted to outfits that are simple, stylish, and unfussy. Ariens are impatient, and you like to be able to change clothes quickly. Red tends to be a favorite color and adds a dynamic splash that really suits your personality. Arien women may prefer to wear pants a lot of the time, because you can feel a bit uncomfortable in a skirt or dress. You might also be reluctant to use too much makeup.

When dressing up, male Ariens look good in formal outfits that do much to reflect their athletic physique. You certainly like to look manly! For women, a special occasion is an opportunity to look better than everyone else, and you love to attract attention with a stylish and sexy image that will probably involve purchasing a new outfit and the latest perfume.

LIFESTYLE CHOICES

The Arien need for space and simplicity means that your home is usually an uncluttered one. You like to feel that you can move around from room to room unhindered, and whatever furniture there is tends to be simple and well defined. You prefer clear and direct interior designs,

HEALTH

THE average Aries is favored with an extremely strong constitution, which means that you will shrug off most minor complaints with ease. Your busy workload is liable to make you overdo it physically at times, and this is when problems can occur.

Aries rules the head, and many of you suffer from headaches and migraines, especially when under stress. Your fiery nature also makes you prone to fevers, but these will generally be intense and short-lived. If you become ill, you tend to rush back on your feet and sometimes prolong recovery by doing so before you are ready.

Your active lifestyle makes you vulnerable to accidents, particularly when you are tired and run down. Meanwhile, living at a fast pace can mean skipping main meals and snacking on junk food, which causes problems with your digestion. Make sure you have a healthy, balanced diet, with plenty of fresh produce—you need the best possible fuel for your body.

When you are young, you may take your robust health for granted, but as the years progress, it will become apparent that you are not indestructible after all! For Ariens, therefore, a little foresight has its benefits.

▲ This 18-century depiction of Aries is one of a series of zodiacal signs at the impressive Jantar Mantar astronomical observatory, Jaipur, India.

often with bold color schemes that don't take too long to paint. You like to create a bright, fresh atmosphere, and will often sleep with the window open, even in the middle of winter.

Because you are so physically active and like doing things for yourself, many Ariens are extremely practical, and carry out their own home and car maintenance. However, although you will probably have green thumbs, gardening is not something that appeals to you all that much. If it does, you tend to be interested in plants that grow as quickly as possible.

Your competitive nature means that your home is often a showcase for your success in life. As you progress in your career, you will happily invest in your home to reflect your increasing status. Although you are friendly toward your neighbors, you won't put up with any annoying behavior from them. Many Ariens have such a busy lifestyle that your home will often function simply as a place that you visit occasionally. Most Ariens have a real ability for making money. However, your impulsive and active nature can find it hard to hold onto it!

Because you live very much on a day-to-day basis, taking a long-term view is hard for you. A life-insurance plan is unlikely to appeal when you are young. Some Ariens like money for the freedom it offers, and others like it for the power it brings. You can be generous, but you will always look after number one.

EXERCISE

REGULAR and vigorous exercise is very important to the typical Arien. Sports offer the perfect outlets to channel your abundant physical energy. Your desire for adventure and excitement can lead you to take an interest in more risky activities such as mountain climbing (right), parachuting, and motor racing. Many Ariens are drawn to the martial arts—judo, karate, and kung fu, for example—as these activities provide the sort of demanding challenge you like. Fast and energetic pursuits, such as running, swimming, and cycling, are also very popular. You are driven by a need to compete, so whichever sport you choose, you will enter it with utter enthusiasm, determined to be the best in the shortest possible time.

If you are not earning enough cash from your work, you quickly seek other avenues. Taking a second job or starting your own business are both popular choices. You are extremely creative, and it's relatively easy for most Ariens to begin a business project of some kind. The question is, however, will it last? You get so restless and bored that many good ideas tend to go to waste. However, for an Aries—man or woman—the rewards of being your own boss are so great that many of you manage to overcome your initial impatience.

When it comes to investment, you should avoid any get-rich-quick schemes. Most Ariens learn the hard way in this matter and, after a few false starts, you eventually realize that success simply cannot be forced. Maintaining regular savings becomes enjoyable after the initial funds have been built up.

ARIENS AT PLAY

As well as playing sports, many Ariens love games. Your desire to win gives you the necessary motivation to practice and persist. Aries being the most active sign, you prefer to spend your leisure time doing something. Lazing around and taking it easy just isn't you. Most Ariens love driving for pleasure, and will often go for a drive simply to unwind at the end of a long day. You like going fast and can be reckless, so you have more near-accidents than others. Books and films have to be fast-paced to hold your interest.

You eat out quite a lot, and are adventurous when eating, and hot, spicy food is especially popular. You also love to party, and periodically you burn the candle at both ends. The typical Aries adores travel, and you will have as many vacations as your budget allows. Your need for adventure is fulfilled by exploring other cultures, and you are not opposed to roughing it if need be.

Standing around waiting is liable to make you irritable; time is of the essence and should not be wasted. You prefer shopping to meet your needs as they arise. Having to plan carefully for the future can be very constricting for you.

Above all else, you have strong principles, and feel actions speak louder than words. Ariens dislike cowardly behavior, and you will go out of your way to confront problems head-on. You find that your energy wanes when life gets too complicated. In general, clarity and purpose make an Aries happy.

THE PERFECT LOVE MATCH

Discover how Ariens fare in relationships with other star signs

Sign	Match	Rating
Aries	Unstable fireworks	❤❤❤
Taurus	Dull and predictable	❤
Gemini	Stimulating fun	❤❤❤❤
Cancer	Too emotional	❤❤
Leo	Strong, passionate love	❤❤❤❤
Virgo	No understanding	❤
Libra	Winning partnership	❤❤❤❤❤
Scorpio	Good as an affair	❤❤❤
Sagittarius	Fire sign perfection	❤❤❤❤❤
Capricorn	Don't bother	❤❤
Aquarius	A laid-back combo	❤❤❤❤
Pisces	Unfocused	❤❤

TAURUS APRIL 20–MAY 20

Those born under the Sun sign of Taurus are strong willed with a down-to-earth attitude toward life. You have a real need for security and will feel unsettled unless you are comfortable on both a material and emotional level. Taureans like to have every aspect of their world running in a regular rhythm, and are instinctively in tune with natural cycles. Your easygoing and earthy nature gives you great potential for happiness. However, your gentle manner sometimes belies your determination to achieve your goals.

Taureans are probably the most patient sign of the zodiac! If you feel something is worthwhile, then you are prepared to wait for it, no matter how long it takes.

Because money is important to you, a lot of your energy will be spent making sure that you are financially secure. Taureans work extremely hard in their pursuit of wealth. You are interested in material things, and possessions of all kinds appeal to you. Whatever it is that you are buying, quality is a prime concern. Most Taureans avoid cheaply made, inferior goods, and would rather spend more to get something

▲ Taurus is associated with The Hierophant in tarot, which represents convention and conformity. The card is also associated with the role of teacher.

▶ A detail from Gerard Mercator's celestial globe of 1551, showing the constellation of Taurus. The globe is on display in the Harvard Map Collection.

Oculus ♉, Palilicium Rom:
Aldebaran, regia Car:
regia Card.
Alfon
Alfo
Alfon
Bella
trix
TAVRVS

TRADITIONAL ASSOCIATIONS Taureans are most closely associated with the following:	
COLORS:	Green and pink
COUNTRIES:	Iran, Ireland, Cyprus
TAROT CARD:	Number 5, the Hierophant
FLOWERS:	Rose
BIRTHSTONE:	Emerald, topaz
ANIMALS:	Bull, elephant
OCCUPATIONS:	Farmer, florist, banker, cosmetician
HERBS:	Mint
TREES:	Almond, apple, plum
CITIES:	Dublin, Leipzig, St. Louis
FOOD:	Potatoes, chocolate

of lasting value. Sometimes you take this materialistic outlook to extremes, obtaining all your emotional security from money and possessions. This can hinder the way you relate to others, however.

Your requirements from life are generally very basic; as well as material success, a solid relationship is very important. Taureans are very physical, and enjoy life to the fullest. A secure home and fulfilling job, good food and wine, and someone to share it with go a long way toward making you happy. Taureans are well adapted to living in the world, and derive lasting satisfaction from the simple things in life.

THE TAUREAN MAN

The typical Taurean male has a somewhat stocky appearance, with a noticeably thick neck. You have naturally well-developed muscles, and this solid physical presence will show itself no matter how much clothing you are wearing. As you walk you take slow, deliberate steps, your large feet connecting well with the ground.

Solid, dependable, and practical, you like to know where you stand in the world. Taureans take a long-term view perspective. Your career is extremely important, as it provides the material platform for success in other areas of your life. Once you have your mind set on achieving something, nothing will distract you from reaching your goal.

Taureans are essentially placid, but you can react with surprising strength of purpose when pushed. You don't lose your temper easily, but when you do, others had better watch out! You have strong opinions and cling to these quite tenaciously, even when they work against you. Taureans are also averse to change, and you sometimes miss great opportunities because of this.

Having a partner is necessary for you to feel complete as a man, although you do need to feel financially secure before getting married and setting up a home.

▲ Taureans are associated with roses. Different colors have different meanings, with red signifying love.

THE TAUREAN WOMAN

Taurean women are very sensual. They tend to have full, rounded figures that convey a healthy, physical look, rosy cheeks, and beautiful, lustrous hair. Like Taurean men, you walk with slow, solid strides that give an impression of being in touch with the ground.

You have a strong sense of right and wrong, and can be very uncompromising in living up to your own standards. Taurus is a very moral sign, displaying real courage in following principles. Being so practical in most areas of life, your head will usually rule your heart. You are romantic, but your material needs are also very strong, and you simply won't be happy or at peace unless these criteria are satisfied.

▲ Emeralds stand for truthfulness—something Taureans value highly.

You have a commonsense approach to life, and tend to dislike fussy, complicated situations. Taureans are very grounded on the whole, and are therefore good in a crisis. It takes a lot to truly unnerve you. You are physically tough, and are able to work for long periods without rest.

You enjoy earthly pleasures, however, and have no trouble indulging your deep sensuality. Colors and textures are very important to you, and you have a deep appreciation of the finer things in life. Although you can easily live on your own, a stable relationship with someone you trust gives you the security you need in order to really blossom.

DRESS SENSE

Both sexes tend to dress conventionally — you don't like presenting an image that is too unusual. Taureans view clothes as an investment, and are happy to spend hard-earned cash on classic, quality items that will last, as your self-worth is enhanced by having expensive outfits that look good.

Most Taureans prefer natural fabrics, and will avoid synthetics wherever possible. As a result, cottons and silks are real favorites. Most Taurean women love floral patterns, and generally seek work and casual clothes with a rich, sensuous appeal. You love the feeling of luxury next to your skin! You also like rich beauty creams and perfumes of all sorts, especially those with strong aromas.

Male Taureans prefer traditional styles, and are very comfortable in a suit. If you have the funds, it will be expertly tailored, as you regard this as a worthwhile investment. All Taureans choose office wear that is smart, functional, and classy. Making the right impression both socially and at work is very important to you; although you appreciate clothes in their own right, you also like to show that you can afford the best labels. Dressing up gives you a chance to bring out the finest outfits in your wardrobe.

For more casual attire, you favor relatively simple, natural designs. Above all, you want to feel comfortable and relaxed, and often enjoy hanging around in a pair of jeans and a T-shirt.

HEALTH

MANY Taureans have difficulties with their weight. You love good food and wine, and this is often consumed in large quantities. But your metabolism can be sluggish, and your easygoing manner does little to burn off all those calories. In later years, it may be necessary to watch what you eat, but most Taureans have a very resilient constitution that can carry extra pounds. When you do become ill, you are able to fight with tremendous strength and determination, often recovering through willpower alone.

The parts of the body most closely related to Taurus are the neck and the throat, and this is one area where health problems can occur. Infections range from mild sore throats to laryngitis and swollen glands.

You are also prone to stiff necks, which are usually the result of tension that has accumulated over a period of time. You like to stay calm, and as a result, can sometimes repress feelings of anger and stress.

Taureans always gain much from letting off steam through some sort of physical activity. This is also a surefire way of combatting the debilitating effects of your sometimes all-too-sedentary lifestyle.

▲ This marble rendition of Taurus dates from the early 18th century and can be found in the Basilica of St. Mary of the Angels and the Martyrs in Rome.

LIFESTYLE CHOICES

A secure, comfortable home is very important to a Taurean's sense of well-being. You like big, solid, traditional buildings that look like they were built to last. As soon as you are able, you invest in an apartment or house, and take great pleasure from owning your own home. Many Taureans have a natural affinity for the country, and if you can't actually live there, you will do your best to have a garden.

You love chunky furniture made out of natural materials, such as wood and leather. Substantial pine tables, sumptuous beds, and luxurious leather sofas are items found in many Taurean homes. Gradually, you will fill your house with valuable objects, and appliances, such as a washing machine and refrigerator, will be the best you can afford.

When it comes to interior designs, you like pastel shades, and enjoy painting and selecting attractive fabrics for curtains and rugs. Floral prints are a common theme, and these are often complemented with flowers, preferably from your own garden!

Money matters are extremely important to Taureans. At an early age, you are aware of its effect on your sense of security. Many Taurus children keep full piggy banks! You have an astute financial brain and find it easy to balance the books. You like dealing with money, which is why, for so many Taureans, investment becomes an enjoyable and profitable hobby.

EXERCISE

UNLESS they absolutely have to, most Taureans avoid strenuous exercise of any kind altogether. With this being the case, attempts to keep your weight down may find you working out in the gym, but otherwise you prefer gardening (right) or going for a long walk. Motivation for both will likely be increased if you are lucky enough to live in the countryside.

Taurean women often express an interest in dancing and yoga, especially when they realize how much their figures benefit from the stretching that these activities involve.

Male Taureans sometimes like to use their natural physical prowess in wrestling and boxing, although most of you would rather be involved as spectators than performers!

Your methodical and pragmatic approach shows itself in the sort of investments you choose. Long-term viability is a priority, since you want to make sure that you and your loved ones are financially secure in the years to come. You are a natural with the stock market, and select safe stocks that you have researched meticulously beforehand.

If you have the funds, you like to express your artistic side, and will buy art and antiques that not only look good but will eventually increase in value. Many Taureans become quite wealthy at some point in their lives. However, rather than just hoarding money for its own sake, you also like using it to get the maximum enjoyment out of life. Friends and family around you certainly benefit frequently from your generosity.

TAUREANS AT PLAY

Taureans know how to enjoy life, and make the most of any leisure time. Resting and taking it easy is something that comes naturally to you, and you like to relax by watching TV, reading, and listening to your favorite music. Sometimes Taureans are prone to periods of laziness, however, and find it hard to motivate themselves.

Going out to dinner with friends is something you like to do as often as you can. Taureans make good cooks, but you certainly appreciate the luxury of having someone else do all the work.

Taureans are also well known for their love of gardening: Caring for plants—inside and outside of the home—gives you a profound sense of satisfaction. You are also passionate about music, and may even have a talent for singing yourself. At the very least, you will not think twice about investing in a good sound system.

Your music taste ranges from classical, particularly opera, to the more thumping sounds of modern music. Being artistic, Taureans are also drawn to painting and pottery. You love working with the sensuous textures of paints and clay.

Taureans like routines, and adjusting to change can be difficult. You love pleasure, and will repeat the same experiences, enjoying each time as much as the last. You are not one for huge surprises, although a thoughtful gift is welcome. Taureans like to go at their own pace, and you resent people who want to hurry you.

Poverty is upsetting for most Taureans, and a healthy bank balance helps you to sleep soundly at night.

THE PERFECT LOVE MATCH

Discover how Taureans fare in relationships with other star signs

Sign	Match	Rating
Aries	Too fiery	❤❤
Taurus	All or nothing	❤❤❤❤❤
Gemini	Flighty	❤
Cancer	Deep love	❤❤❤❤
Leo	Once in a while	❤❤❤
Virgo	Earth sign delight	❤❤❤❤❤
Libra	Possible	❤❤❤
Scorpio	Opposites attract	❤❤❤❤
Sagittarius	No way!	❤
Capricorn	Seriously good	❤❤❤❤❤
Aquarius	Mismatch	❤❤❤
Pisces	Sweet and loving	❤❤❤❤

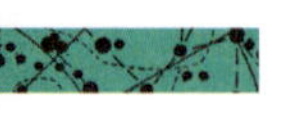

GEMINI MAY 21–JUNE 20

Geminis are restless, and your active brains need almost constant mental stimulation. This means that in virtually all areas of your life, you seek a wide variety of contrasting experiences. Boredom is to be avoided at all costs! Curious and alert, you love communicating with others around you, and never run out of things to talk about. Your versatile mind picks up facts quickly, and you love acquiring knowledge. So many topics interest you that you risk only gaining a rather superficial understanding of several subjects.

It is difficult for a Geminian to concentrate for a long period of time, and this is one reason why many of you find it hard to maintain a consistent lifestyle.

Gemini is a complex sign; the twins represent the inherent duality of your nature. Your two halves need contrasts, and you feel uncomfortable without them. You thrive on nervous energy and love being busy. Geminis will typically read more than one book at the same time, hold down two or three jobs, study something new at night school, and still have energy for a hectic social schedule that may or may not include a partner.

▲ Gemini is associated with The Lovers card in tarot, which represents love relationships, romance, feelings, harmony, and perfection.

▶ Entitled Twins, Signs of the Zodiac, this rendition of Gemini appeared in a 15th-century **Atlas Celeste** (Star Atlas). The artist is unknown.

TRADITIONAL ASSOCIATIONS

Geminians are most closely associated with the following:

COLORS:	Yellow, black, white
COUNTRIES:	Armenia, Belgium, Sardinia
TAROT CARD:	Number 6, The Lovers
FLOWERS:	Lily of the Valley
BIRTHSTONE:	Tourmaline, agate
ANIMALS:	Magpie, small birds
OCCUPATIONS:	Writer, TV presenter, journalist
HERBS:	Caraway
TREES:	Nut-bearing trees
CITIES:	Bruges, San Francisco, New York, Nuremberg
FOOD:	Nuts and seeds

On a deep level, this fragmentation is a reflection of your search to integrate your many selves. As you get older you discover one or two things that you really want to focus on, and these bring much happiness and contentment. You will always retain a youthfulness that enables you to look at the world with fresh eyes. Sometimes called the Peter Pan of the zodiac, you relate well to children; preferring to stay childlike yourself, you avoid heavy commitments. Geminians never stop learning, and provided you find constructive outlets for your immense mental energy, life will always be rewarding and full of interest.

THE GEMINIAN MAN

The Gemini male is normally tall and lean. He walks at a brisk pace, looking around as he goes. You are agile, and your eyes convey the curiosity for which your sign is famous. Geminians age slowly, and generally appear much younger than their years.

For many Gemini men, life is one big adventure, and you find it hard to resist any new experience. Ever curious, your need for stimulation takes you down some fascinating roads, and you often end up flirting with danger. You want to taste so much of life that it's just as well that you are clever and persuasive, as you are able to use your charm to great advantage. You are intelligent and witty, and need positive mental challenges to stop you from getting bored too quickly.

You are unlikely to settle down for some time, as you feel there are too many things you want to do before making commitments. As you go through phases and explore the many different parts of your nature, you need the freedom to be able to move on and adapt. This can mean a steady succession of jobs, girlfriends, and places to live, and you're too busy enjoying yourself to notice what you are leaving behind. Gemini men will find fulfillment through living life on your own terms, in a way others respect.

THE GEMINIAN WOMAN

The Gemini woman is usually tall, slender with bright, penetrating eyes. You move quickly, with small, neat steps. When talking to others you are animated, and use your hands to make gestures. Like the men, you are youthful, and your face expresses a childlike curiosity.

The Gemini woman is multifaceted, and you need to express as many sides of your personality as possible. You have a very good mind, and love to use it. A career is important from an early age and you will probably change direction every so often. But you enjoy working and benefit from the feeling of security that it gives. Gemini women like to study, and you often take courses in order to learn new skills.

▲ Gemini's flower, lily of the valley, represents humility, chastity, and purity and is said to bring luck in love.

▲ Agate enhances creativity and is said to balance yin/yang energy.

You are independent, and love being out on the town, generally having a very active social life. Keeping up with the latest fashions, you resist getting old before your time, making a determined effort to stay young. This can make it hard for you to settle down, although you are more prepared to take on commitments than a Gemini man. You are romantic, but many relationships may come and go before you find someone who meets your requirements for a lasting bond.

DRESS SENSE

The Geminian love of variety will express itself in your choice of clothes. You portray different images according to your mood, and others are amazed by the contrasting styles that you wear. Sometimes it takes friends a little while to realize who it is! Textures, colors, and accessories are regularly combined with great success. However, Geminians do have to fight a tendency to mix too many styles at once, resulting in real clashes.

You love to shop for up-to-date clothes; magazines are a great source of ideas, to which you add your own inventive twists. Geminians know all the best places to shop, and some of the items you buy cost a fortune, while others are dirt cheap. When it comes to accessories, you are a bit of a collector and love to scour flea markets for interesting and useful bargains.

Gemini women look especially good in classic clothes that show off their lithe and youthful figures. You probably have many pairs of shoes, some of them hardly worn. Varied accessories are also popular as you need to feel choices are available when preparing to go out.

Male Geminians steer clear of clothes that make them look too staid and conventional. You have a boyish charm, and select items that help you maintain your youthful image. Both sexes can refuse to grow old gracefully, wearing outfits that are designed for someone much younger. But most Geminians avoid this, as your adaptable nature helps you look great whatever your age.

LIFESTYLE CHOICES

Even if you don't spend much time at home, you like to be able to keep up your restless

HEALTH

GEMINIANS have a lot of energy. Your metabolism is fast and you burn many calories. Provided you pay attention to the demands of your body, you will enjoy above average health.

However, Geminians possess delicate nervous systems, and sometimes you lead life at such a hectic pace that there is a danger that you will become very tense and stressed out. It is important that you remember to slow down and take time to relax, and also make the effort to have regular meals. You will probably require more sleep than others, as your sensitive nerves need time to regenerate thoroughly.

The lungs are a potential weak point for Geminians, and a cold can result in a nasty lingering cough. Wrap up against the elements, and perhaps take vitamins when winter arrives. The other areas of the body related to Gemini are the shoulders, arms, and hands. These are vulnerable to injury, and sprains or broken bones may occur at some stage in your life.

When you do suffer from ill health, you are a reluctant patient and will try to make light of your misfortune. Geminians recover fairly quickly, and it takes a serious illness to stop you from being restless.

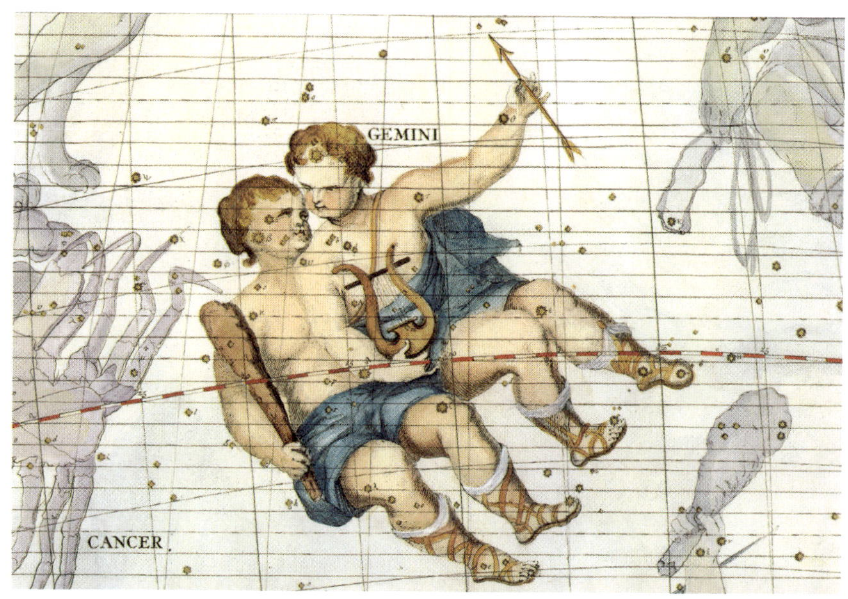

and varied lifestyle when you are there. Communication is vitally important, and you use your phone a lot. Computers are popular and you will have a good selection of books, newspapers, and magazines. The TV is often on, if only in the background. Most Geminians like technology and your living environment may be full of the latest utility and leisure appliances.

The general atmosphere of the Geminian home is bright and lively, with stimulating color schemes and a clever use of space and light. Rooms frequently have more than one function, which reflects your ability to adapt. You have versatile furniture that can be easily moved, and you rearrange rooms whenever you feel like a change.

For most Geminians, location is more of a concern than the type of property. You like to be near the action; the hustle and bustle of a large metropolis is very attractive. Many Geminis get bored living in the countryside, and sooner or later move into an urban environment. If you can, you find accommodation in the hippest part of town. Here you have access to an interesting variety of places to eat and shop, and, of course, plenty of night life.

▲ An engraving of the constellation of Gemini from John Flamsteed's **Atlas Coelestis**, published in 1729, hand-colored by the artist, James Thornhill.

Geminians can find it hard to hold onto their cash. You make money easily, and often have more than one source of income; however, you also love spending money! Geminis are never at a loss for things to do and buy, as your interests are constantly evolving.

EXERCISE

GEMINIANS usually live off their nerves, and can easily neglect their health as a result. You are mentally active almost all of the time, and sometimes it can be hard for you to switch off. Consider practicing meditation and gentle forms of Eastern movement, such as yoga and t'ai chi, as these offer a way of helping you to discover a certain degree of serenity.

You gain much from regular physical exercise (right). It helps you to stay relaxed, and puts you in touch with your body. Of all the sports available to you, you enjoy tennis and squash most, and prefer exercising in a social environment—joining a health club and working out with others is a lot more fun that going for a solitary run or scaling a rockface.

The boring, practical details involved with finance are difficult for you to take seriously. This can be a problem, as sometimes you may fail to keep your affairs in order. You have the funds, but you don't always use them well, since you are too busy getting on with the rest of your life!

A Geminian standard of living can fluctuate rapidly, as you may not know what you will be doing from one year to the next. Sometimes you use credit cards and loans to supplement your earnings, and can run up quite large debts without realizing it. Being organized is the key to financial success for the typical Geminian.

Investments work well if they are fun and can keep you interested. You are usually quick to spot opportunities and can make remarkably shrewd judgments, especially when you use your inquiring mind to read up on the subject.

GEMINIANS AT PLAY

Geminians love communicating, and you often spend time talking to others on your cell phone. Reading and writing appeal, and you will sit for hours composing letters. Words fascinate you; Scrabble and crosswords are favorite pastimes. For many Geminians, spare time is an opportunity to study, and you have a talent for picking up languages quickly.

Going out with friends gives you great pleasure, and you usually belong to a very active social circle. Bars, clubs, movies, and galleries—you appreciate a wide variety of entertainment, and love sharing it with other stimulating minds.

You are interested in the media, and enjoy keeping up with the news; you are an ideal candidate for cable and satellite TV channels. You like technology and many Geminians derive tremendous enjoyment from their computer, especially the Internet. Global information 24 hours a day is a Gemini's idea of heaven!

You need variety, contrast, and change, and feel restricted and frustrated if you don't get it. To break up your normal routine, you enjoy short breaks, perhaps staying with friends. You are not happy spending long periods of time by yourself, as Geminians thrive on companionship. Having nothing to do really gets you down, and you will go out of your way to keep busy and avoid boredom.

You start to feel trapped if you are forced to make too many commitments, as you prefer to keep your options open, always keeping one eye on the horizon.

THE PERFECT LOVE MATCH

Discover how Geminians fare in relationships with other star signs

Aries	Lasting passion	❤❤❤❤
Taurus	You must be kidding!	❤❤
Gemini	Will it last?	❤❤❤❤
Cancer	Possible...	❤❤❤
Leo	True love	❤❤❤❤
Virgo	Surprising success	❤❤❤❤
Libra	Relaxing winner	❤❤❤❤❤
Scorpio	Too intense	❤
Sagittarius	Opposites attract	❤❤❤
Capricorn	Most unlikely	❤
Aquarius	Soul mates	❤❤❤❤❤
Pisces	Too dreamy	❤

CANCER JUNE 21–JULY 22

Cancerians are known for having a tough, shell-like exterior that protects their very sensitive and vulnerable personalities from the world outside. Really, you're quite a softy, and because you have such delicate emotions, you need to feel safe. That is why you sometimes behave defensively. You find it hard to be direct, preferring to approach things from an angle, advancing gradually. Once you have committed yourself to a course of action, however, you display great tenacity in reaching your goal, often to the surprise of those around you.

▲ Cancer is associated with The Chariot card in tarot, which has much to do with change and movement. It can also represent success or progress.

▶ Detail from "Cancer" as depicted in **Urania's Mirror**, a set of 32 constellation cards engraved by Sidney Hall and published in London ca 1825.

Family life is very important, and most Cancerians are extremely close to their next of kin—indeed, it is hard for you to feel secure unless relationships at home are good. Your childhood is always remembered, and it is here that you develop your instinctive need to care, which sooner or later will express itself in most areas of your life. You are so attached to the past that you sometimes fail to take advantage of current opportunities, and can have a tendency to dwell in nostalgia.

Cancerians are emotional and intuitive, with an almost psychic ability to pick up on how people are feeling and what

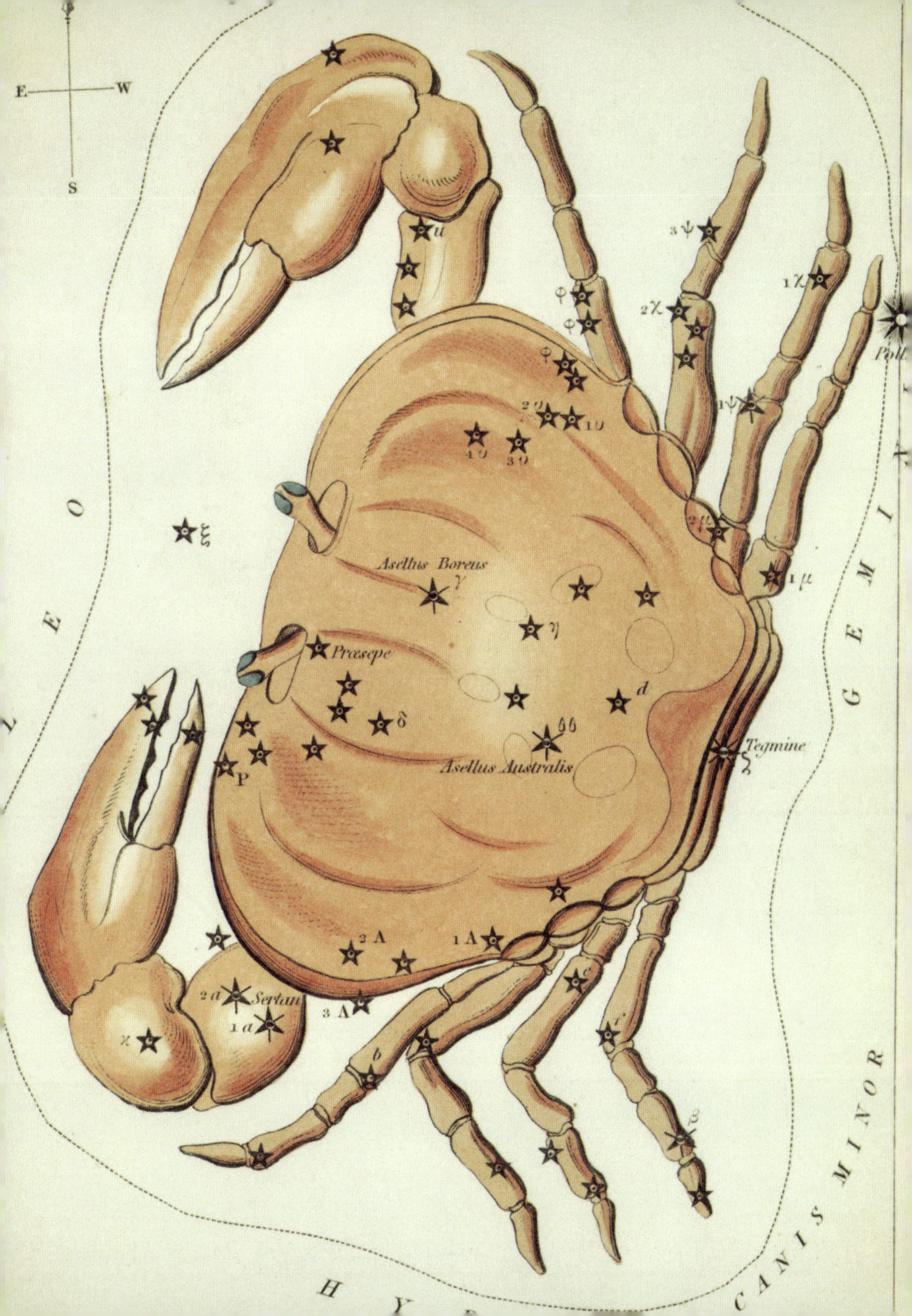

E
W
S
LEO
Asellus Boreus
Præsepe
Asellus Australis
Tegmine
CANIS MINOR

TRADITIONAL ASSOCIATIONS

Cancerians are most closely associated with the following:

COLORS:	Silver, indigo
COUNTRIES:	Canada, The Netherlands, United States
TAROT CARD:	Number 7, The Chariot
FLOWERS:	Lotus
BIRTHSTONE:	Moonstone, pearl
ANIMALS:	Crabs, frogs
OCCUPATIONS:	Nurse, antique dealer, chef, interior designer
HERBS:	Lemon balm
TREES:	Alder, willow
CITIES:	Istanbul, Venice, Amsterdam
FOOD:	Shellfish, lettuce, mushrooms

is going on in their minds. You are also strongly attuned to nature, and care deeply about the environment, becoming very upset by man-made and natural disasters. Cancerians are complex, with many changing moods that can be difficult for others to fathom. One minute you will be sulky and withdrawn, and the next, kind and affectionate. Once you learn to deal with your extreme sensitivity, it becomes an asset, and allows you to have a rich and emotionally fulfilling life.

THE CANCERIAN MAN

The Cancerian man is inclined to be a little on the plump side; you have a round, moon-shaped face that conveys a variety of changing expressions. Dimples are common, and you have a ready smile. Your eyes are usually kind and sensitive, but you sometimes find it hard to meet the gaze of others. You have a strong need for security, and will feel emotionally out of sorts if you don't have a comfortable place to live and money in your pocket. Cancerians have a very strong sense of privacy, and are usually extremely cautious when it comes to opening up to others, which is why a solid home base is absolutely fundamental to your well-being.

Many Cancerian men remain very attached to their mothers, and like to keep a close emotional bond for as long as they possibly can. You are very creative and intuitive in nature, and frequently make decisions—even important ones—based on your gut feelings. These usually turn out to be right, although you are sometimes guilty of waiting too long before acting on them.

Having a family is something you will want to do at some stage. Cancerian men are very domesticated, and most women find this attractive. Ideally suited to the roles of husband and father, your business acumen ensures that everyone is well taken care of.

THE CANCERIAN WOMAN

Like Cancerian men, you have eyes that reveal a lot of emotion, and an expressive, often moon-shaped face. Your bone structure is generally strong, and according to your mood, you either slouch or carry yourself with an upright posture. Your body weight fluctuates, and you are often amply proportioned.

Cancerian women are generally ruled by their emotions, and you obtain much security through having close contact with friends and family members. You can find it very frustrating if you are unable to express your caring nature, and get depressed if this goes on for a long time without change. You are touchy and sensitive, and are quick to take offense, even though none may have been intended.

▲ The lotus flower is significant in many world religions and is said to symbolize inner purity and harmony.

▲ The pearl is often considered a symbol of purity and innocence.

Creative and highly imaginative, you have a talent for all forms of design. Cancerians are influenced by their subconscious, and your deep intuition gives you much insight into human nature. You have a strong sense of self-preservation, and use this for guidance when making decisions.

Cancerians are very maternal, and possess a strong nesting instinct. Although you will probably have a successful career, you appreciate an intimate relationship more than most, and love having children and running a family home.

DRESS SENSE

Cancerians can have problems in discovering what sort of look suits them best, as you choose clothes according to your mood. When it comes to actually buying new outfits to wear, you can be reluctant to spend too much money, and will wait for as long as possible before renewing items in your wardrobe. Cancerians are shrewd, and quite content to wear hand-me-downs, often maximizing the overall effect with the addition of one or two carefully chosen accessories.

Although you have a great sense of color and texture, you avoid dressing in a manner that attracts attention, preferring to create a subtle and slightly understated image. With your interest in the past, current fashion may leave you cold, and most Cancerians opt for traditional and conventional styles. Males can be surprisingly fussy about their appearance, and may take some time to get ready before going out. You favor well-cut suits and comfortable, stylish casuals. Sporty items are rarely worn, and you often look good in clothes with a nautical theme.

For work, women like dress suits, which help you feel comfortable and efficient. When relaxing, you prefer feminine clothes with gentle, flowing lines. Dressing up is romantic, and you love to go out into the magic of night.

LIFESTYLE CHOICES

To a Cancerian, a home is a haven from the hustle and bustle of the world, a place where you can relax and really be yourself. You will go out of your way to create a cozy and familiar atmosphere there, and

HEALTH

CANCERIANS are very emotional, and your immune system is strongly affected by how you are feeling at any given time. When you are happy, your health will be exceptionally good. However, a bout of depression can leave you susceptible to everything that is going around. Essentially, you possess a tough and resilient constitution, and will recover from even serious illness with ease.

Cancerians usually suffer in silence and rarely protest, despite the fact that you may be in great pain. You respond well to care and affection, as your body and mind are linked so strongly—feeling loved does more than anything else to assist a speedy return to health.

The main part of the body that relates to Cancer is the stomach. When you are upset, your digestion can be impaired, and it may be advisable to wait until you are calm before sitting down to eat. However, in general, you need to eat regular meals, as being hungry will put you in a bad mood, and can make it difficult for you to keep your poise. For most Cancerians, happiness will do more than anything else to ensure good levels of health throughout your life.

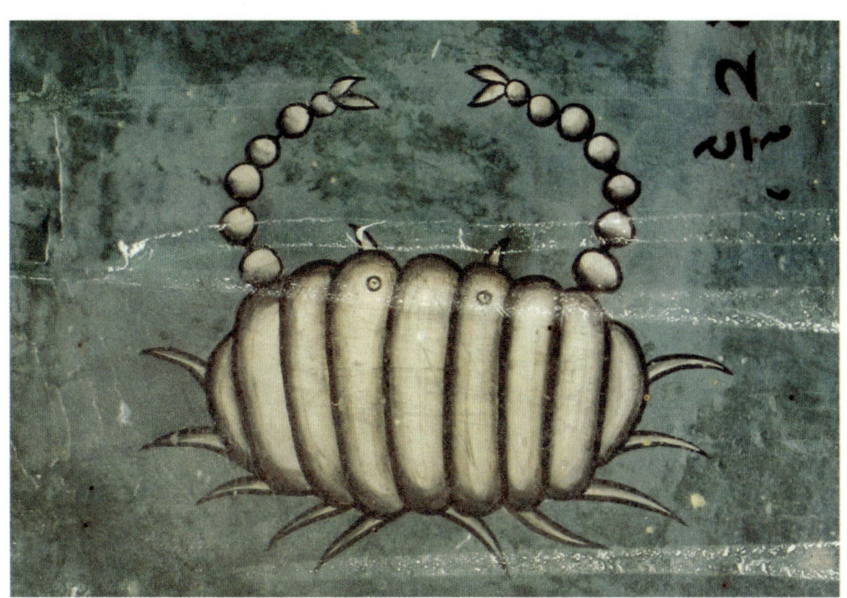

▲ This 18-century depiction of Cancer is one of a series of zodiacal signs at the impressive Jantar Mantar astronomical observatory, Jaipur, India.

are happy to spend a substantial amount of money to achieve this. The outside environment should also be peaceful and many Cancerians live in the country, as modern cities may be too stressful for your sensitive nature. You are drawn to properties that have some kind of history, and also like living near water.

All Cancerians love collecting things, and you will usually own some lovely pieces of antique furniture that have been acquired over the years. Your passion for antiques often results in large hoards of china and other collectibles that can be positioned rather haphazardly from room to room. Cancerians are not known for their tidiness, and sometimes the overall effect is one of clutter. You love food and cooking, and the kitchen is likely to be large and well equipped. Gardening is another interest, and many of you will indulge your green thumbs. Cancerians are very private and quick to defend your territorial rights, having little patience with nosy, obtrusive neighbors.

Cancerians are extremely cautious when it comes to money. This reflects your deep need to hold on to what you have, making you very careful and shrewd. On occasion, you will even hesitate before buying the simple necessities of life, as not having enough funds leaves you feeling exposed and vulnerable. You like money for the security it offers, and often devote a lot of time and energy to building up a large and substantial bank balance.

EXERCISE

CANCERIANS will always benefit tremendously from regular exercise, as this helps you to relax and tends to counter your anxiety.

You are especially attracted to water sports, particularly swimming. You like peaceful environments, however, and may prefer to arrive at the swimming pool early, before the crowds get there. You are the kind of person that, once comfortable with a set exercise routine, you tend to stick to it for many years to come. Getting close to nature is popular with Cancerians (right), and many of you enjoy hiking, cycling, and camping—often in large wildernesses. These are particularly good pastimes for you, as Cancerians need periods of solitude in order to recharge their batteries fully.

Cancerians are financially intuitive, and usually possess remarkable business acumen. Unless you have great respect for an expert, you would much rather keep control of your own financial affairs. Investments of all sorts appeal, but you will generally steer well clear of anything that appears risky and unpredictable. Many of you supplement your regular income with a hobby, such as buying and selling antiques, or some other form of trade. Your judgment is superb, and many profitable careers spring from such ventures. As you get increasingly wealthy, you relax, and are more able to enjoy the good things in life, sharing these with family members and close friends.

CANCERIANS AT PLAY

Because Cancerians love antiques and collecting so much, you may spend at least some of your free time rummaging around flea markets and yard sales, hoping to find something interesting to buy. If your hobby is more serious, your face will be a familiar sight at local auctions.

Cooking is usually one of your favorite pastimes, and you love to invite close friends over for a meal. Cancerians use a lot of creative energy when preparing food, and you like to add your own ideas to enhance established recipes. When you are feeling tense, cooking has a very relaxing effect, and does much to help you unwind. Cancerians also enjoy sailing and boating, as you have a natural affinity with water, and many of you like to go off on a fishing trip once in a while.

Being such a homebody, you are surprisingly fond of travel, and many of you have motor homes so you can take all your creature comforts with you! Cancerians are very close to their relatives, and love to share free time and leisure activities with family members of all ages, especially when it comes to vacationing somewhere abroad.

You are very protective and defensive of your immediate family members, and tend to react strongly to anyone who dares to criticize them. Cancerians have wonderful memories, and you appreciate birthday cards and people who remember special dates and anniversaries.

Cancerians tend to be shy; loud and extrovert displays from others can make you feel too self-conscious. If you live in a noisy location, this can also grate on your nerves, as more than anything else you need a tranquil home base.

THE PERFECT LOVE MATCH

Discover how Cancerians fare in relationships with other star signs

Aries	Steamy affair	♥♥
Taurus	Earthy winner	♥♥♥♥
Gemini	Overly logical	♥
Cancer	Deep love	♥♥♥♥♥
Leo	Possible	♥♥♥
Virgo	Versatile bond	♥♥♥♥
Libra	Different love concepts	♥♥
Scorpio	Caring soul mates	♥♥♥♥♥
Sagittarius	No way!	♥♥
Capricorn	Lasting lovers	♥♥♥♥♥
Aquarius	Too detached	♥
Pisces	Nonstop romance	♥♥♥♥♥

LEO JULY 23–AUGUST 22

Leos tend to be majestic and proud, and have a larger-than-life personality that needs to shine. You want to be in charge, and use passion and vitality to greet opportunities with great enthusiasm. You are an extrovert with a tremendous love for life—a normal, humdrum existence is sure to disappoint you, whatever your age. You need plenty of drama and color in your life! Leos have very strong desires, and once you have set your mind on something, you display a burning determination to make sure that you always get your wish.

This stubbornness can be your downfall, however, as Leos do not like changing course and, consequently, they occasionally persevere with a plan of action that is doomed to fail.

You have strong opinions on most subjects, and voice them with authority. Leos have a natural bravado, and you always sound as though you know what you are talking about, even if you don't! Those around you may find you dogmatic, but no one could accuse you of being weak-willed and indecisive.

As the Lion of the zodiac, you like to feel that you are the king of the jungle and

▲ Leo is associated with the Strength card in tarot, which represents such qualities as power, courage, fortitude, and physical ability.

▶ Leo by Dutch scholar Hugo Grotius in his **Syntagma Arateorvm** (1600), currently held at the Peace Palace Library at The Hague, the Netherlands.

TRADITIONAL ASSOCIATIONS

Leos are most closely associated with the following:

COLORS:	Sunny oranges, yellows
COUNTRIES:	France, Turkey, Italy, Bohemia
TAROT CARD:	Number 11, Strength
FLOWERS:	Sunflowers
BIRTHSTONE:	Tiger's eye, ruby
ANIMALS:	Lions, domestic cats, lynx
OCCUPATIONS:	Actor, business executive, model, clothing designer
HERBS:	Marigold
TREES:	Orange, cedar, bay
CITIES:	Rome, Prague, Damascus
FOOD:	Rich meaty foods

command respect from all around you. You cannot stand it when people laugh at you, and your pride is easily hurt. In your own eyes you are a real celebrity, and you will go out of your way to achieve distinction and recognition in at least one area of your life. Leos actually have the potential to be genuine heroes in life, and are extremely brave and courageous. They often achieve greatness in the face of enormous adversity.

Leos are self-possessed, and can often find it hard to let others have their say. You have a fiery strength that needs to be tempered, as sometimes you can simply overwhelm your friends and the people you meet. If you are able to tone down your act once in a while, the world will find that it has much to gain from your warm and generous heart.

THE LEO MAN

Most Leo men have short, broad backs with well-developed muscles. Your hair is often spectacular and curly, just like a lion's mane. You walk with a dignified posture, and always dress to look good and attract admirers. Your voice is strong and commanding, and you are aware of your powerful sex appeal.

Leos are confident and charming on the whole, and you are quite used to getting your own way. You have grand visions and plans, and dislike those with petty, constricting attitudes. A born show-off, you can't resist playing up to any audience that happens to be around, as you crave attention and need to feel loved and wanted. You have a taste for luxurious living, and like to indulge in the best, sometimes rather ostentatiously.

Leos cannot resist the urge to be in control, and you will try and dominate your destiny whenever possible. You have fantastic willpower that gives you every chance of succeeding in this, although you have to watch a tendency to be too hard on yourself and others.

Honest and loyal, you take great pride in keeping your word. You love romance, and often have many admirers before you decide to play the part of a loving husband. Your wife may need to allow you to be the focus of the marriage.

▲ The sunflower signifies great self-confidence and the need to be the center of attention in a crowd.

THE LEO WOMAN

Leo women have slim, sensuous bodies, and are always very well dressed whatever their personal circumstances. Even more than Leo men, your hair will be a real feature, probably with long, abundant curls that cascade down your back. You may have a superior expression, and will also dress to turn heads.

Leos have a genuine lust for life and demand the very best that it has to offer. You will fight tooth and nail to get it, believing that luxury befits your regal nature. You need recognition and adulation from others, and want them to respond to your sunny disposition.

▲ Tiger's eye enhances willpower. It also brings wealth and prosperity.

You are a very passionate person, and find it hard not to show emotion. Most of the time you will be fairly relaxed, but when you do lose your temper, the results can be quite frightening! You have a lot of self-respect, and do not take kindly to being pushed around.

You tend to be outgoing, and love to share excitement and enjoyment with others, as your life force is too strong to keep to yourself. Relationships are very important, and you need a special man who is able to respect your dominant yet feminine personality. You feel most fully alive when you are in love.

DRESS SENSE

Leos always dress to impress, no matter what the occasion! You simply love to look good, and feel enormous satisfaction when others glance in your direction.

You are attracted to showy and often expensive clothes that help you stand out in a crowd. Anonymity is to be avoided at all costs, and if you really want to create a stir, you are quite prepared to spend a considerable amount of money on something that may be worn only once or twice. Sometimes your desire to get noticed results in an image that is rather tacky, but you soon learn from your mistakes. Both men and women like to feel glamorous, and designer labels appeal for formal and casual wear alike.

Leo women like to dress for work in outfits that are smart, sexy, and powerful. You are aware of the different roles in a career environment, and select a style that helps you achieve the desired impact.

You are romantic too, however, and love the drama of a big night out. As well as choosing your finest dress, you like to wear classy perfume, and finish the look with gold jewelry next to your skin. Leos usually bronze under the sun and feel that they look their best with a healthy tan.

Leo men are also concerned with their appearance, and many spend hours grooming themselves, either at home or at the barbershop. As you dislike looking unkempt, investing money on quality clothes is a real priority.

HEALTH

YOU have a strong constitution that gives much protection against minor infections and complaints. Leos often take their health for granted, and you have to be careful of pushing yourself and working and playing so hard that you get run down. If illness does strike, you are genuinely surprised and almost affronted. You enjoy the attention of being a patient, but you also want others to know how strong you are, and make every effort to recover and get out of bed.

The circulatory system is related to the sign of Leo, and when you become angry or stressed, your blood pressure can be high. Too many rich foods exacerbate this problem, and moderation in diet is thus advised. Men in particular are susceptible to heart disease if they persist with an over-indulgent lifestyle, so regular exercise is prudent, and will do much to ensure that later years are trouble-free.

The other main area of the body connected to Leo is the back, and you try to walk as upright as possible. Because of this you can hold a lot of tension in your back muscles, so regular sit-ups or other exercises designed to strengthen lower-back muscles can be very beneficial.

▲ An image of Leo painted in Kraków's Kupa Synagogue, Poland.

LIFESTYLE CHOICES

Leos are very proud, and you will do your best to make your home as splendid as possible. Even if it is quite a humble abode, you manage without fail to create an atmosphere that is warm, welcoming, and a touch showy. You usually make sure that it is sparkling clean, and looking at its best.

You like grand, palatial properties, and will get as big a place as your budget allows. Inside, you will probably have sumptuous furniture and fittings, the more luxurious the better! Lush textures are favored, and you love the feel of a deep, shag-pile carpet under your feet. Having a comfortable pad to relax in is important to you, and you love to entertain your guests in style.

Leos have a rich sense of color, and you prefer bold interior designs, often featuring sunny shades of yellow and orange. A bright interior is a must, as you like your home to get as much light as possible, and may actually get depressed if it is too dark and gloomy. Good heating is another absolute necessity as most Leos have a low tolerance for cold weather. Indeed, some of you are happy only when living in a hot climate.

Leos have a reputation for being extravagant, and you certainly enjoy living it up! Paying attention to detail is not your forte, and this sometimes results in your spending more than you earn. You can find it difficult to tighten your belt when required, and may borrow funds to enable you to carry on with your lavish lifestyle. Leos are attracted to the best, and do not cope well with poverty. Because of this,

EXERCISE

Leos are, by their very nature, extremely determined, and once you have committed yourself to an exercise program you can stick to it religiously. On the other hand, some Leos are lazy! Nevertheless, most usually enjoy expressing themselves through some form of physical activity.

Leos love moving to music; Latin dances (right) and aerobics appeal. Almost all sports are popular, too, and you like to compete with yourself and others, always trying to improve your personal best. Team sports are often preferred, although you may insist on being captain. If caring for your back and posture is a concern for you, it may be a good idea to take on some regular stretching exercises—you will always obtain positive results.

you are prepared to work very hard to attain a good level of material success, and many Leos become rich. Wealth helps you express your passion for life, and you can feel impotent without it.

When it comes to choosing investments, Leos are surprisingly conventional, preferring to put cash into something reliable and steady. You often seek expert advice to help you make the right decision. You have panache, and may invest in flamboyant enterprises, but this is usually when you have already built up substantial funds—and even then it will be very carefully considered. Leos have a natural affinity with the stage, and you may like to get involved with backing a big show. Other areas that you could do well in include paintings and sculptures, and all forms of jewelry.

LEOS AT PLAY

Leos have a tremendous zest for life, and love to go out and have a good time with friends. You love big events with lots of glitter and glamour, and will often unwind with a night on the town. With your sense of drama, the theater and opera are natural choices, and you appreciate the chance to dress up and be seen—if some celebrities are present, so much the better, as you enjoy rubbing shoulders with the stars.

You have a taste for exclusive restaurants that serve gourmet foods and wines, dining whenever possible with friends. Leos do not like eating out alone, as you need companionship. Shopping is another of your favorite pastimes, although you can feel very frustrated if you don't have the money to buy what you want.

Leos often take up rewarding hobbies, and many of you are drawn toward joining an amateur dramatics group. Your creative talents also find fulfillment with painting, sculpture, and jewelry-making, and you can surprise others with your results.

Given the choice, some Leos do nothing more than laze around for hours like a cat! Pleasures of all sorts appeal, and receiving thoughtful and indulgent gifts from those you love makes you purr with real delight.

As you are a real sucker for flattery, an appreciative audience boosts your ego tremendously. Similarly, being ignored is sure to raise your hackles, and you hate being taken for a fool. If someone breaks your trust, your Leo pride may take some time to heal. You need to feel that your life is special, and can struggle if things become too mundane and drab.

THE PERFECT LOVE MATCH

Discover how Leos fare in relationships with other star signs

Aries	Hot stuff!	♥♥♥♥
Taurus	Sometimes…	♥♥♥
Gemini	Stimulating love	♥♥♥♥
Cancer	Complementary	♥♥♥
Leo	Nonstop passion	♥♥♥♥♥
Virgo	Forget it	♥
Libra	Romantic delight	♥♥♥♥
Scorpio	All or nothing	♥♥♥
Sagittarius	Yes!	♥♥♥♥♥
Capricorn	Definitely possible	♥♥♥
Aquarius	Do opposites attract?	♥♥♥
Pisces	Steamy affair	♥♥♥

VIRGO AUGUST 23–SEPTEMBER 22

Virgoans are discriminating, and have a strong desire to serve. You are critical of yourself and others, and often have impossibly high standards. Details matter to you, which is why you strive for perfection. A Virgoan's mind is a powerful tool, and you need to learn how to use it to your advantage. You are helpful and sympathetic, always ready to lend a hand. Virgoans feel connected to humanity and spend much time working for the good of others, tending to put other people's needs before their own—even if it is inappropriate.

Your sharp insight and ability to probe allows you to see things that others miss, but also makes you inclined to worry, which can really hold you back. Self-doubt is your biggest enemy, but once this is conquered, there really is no stopping you. Virgoans have many talents—some of them hidden—and are surprisingly versatile.

Mentally, you can be quite delicate, and for you to feel secure, it is very important for the practical and material side of life to be in order. A good job is a necessity, as is financial stability. Without these, it can be difficult for you to stop worrying.

▲ Virgo is associated with The Hermit card in tarot, which represents wisdom, prudence, and a movement toward spiritual goals.

▶ A marble rendition of Virgo found in the Basilica of St. Mary of the Angels and the Martyrs in Rome. It dates from the early 18th century.

TRADITIONAL ASSOCIATIONS

Virgoans are most closely associated with the following:

COLORS:	Browns and greens
COUNTRIES:	Greece, Switzerland
TAROT CARD:	Number 9, The Hermit
FLOWERS:	Buttercup
BIRTHSTONE:	Peridot, sardonyx
ANIMALS:	Mice, insects
OCCUPATIONS:	Accountant, scientist, teacher, writer
HERBS:	Lavender
TREES:	Elder, nut-bearing trees
CITIES:	Heidelberg, Boston, Baghdad, Geneva
FOOD:	Wheat and rice

Virgo is an often-misunderstood sign, as part of you is concerned with purity and cleanliness, and this can lead to a real obsession with health and hygiene. Indeed, some Virgoans are very prudish, and find all bodily functions distasteful. However, you are also very earthy and sensuous, with a fondness for the pleasures of the flesh and riotous good times with friends—a part of your more uninhibited, wild side that you may be afraid to express. For true happiness, however, you really need to reconcile and integrate these two Virgoan extremes.

THE VIRGOAN MAN

Virgoan men tend to be tall and straight; you walk with an upright posture, and place your feet on the ground with precise, considered steps. Your face has neat features, and you often give the impression of being deep in thought. Virgoans have a reputation for cleanliness, and you often look as though you have just washed and put on fresh clothes.

Virgoan men are pragmatic, and generally your head will rule your heart. You find it hard to relate to overly "mushy" emotions, and as a result, prefer to stay cool and detached. You have a strong sense of responsibility, and are driven to seek fulfillment through your work.

Instinctively, you like to be busy, and your analytical mind needs plenty to keep it occupied. Without constructive outlets, you channel your energy into being negative and critical of the world at large. This is overcome by doing some sort of service, and for many Virgoans, personal happiness is linked to the welfare of

▲ Lavender flowers have long had associations with purity, silence, devotion, and caution.

others. When it comes to getting involved romantically, you can be remarkably self-sufficient, and spend long periods of time on your own. However, falling in love does much to enrich your life.

THE VIRGOAN WOMAN

Virgoan women usually have delicate bodies, and tend to walk with small, dainty steps. Your hair is always neat and well cut, and your dress tends to be immaculate, with fussy attention to detail. The features on your face are often sharp, and when worried, the mouth and eyes can tense up. When relaxed, your whole expression melts, and you look noticeably younger. Although you are shy and appear to be rather meek at times, this masks your inner qualities of determination and courage. In fact, you are often brutally honest, and are under no illusions about what you want out of life and what will make you happy. Furthermore, you are prepared to sever many ties quite ruthlessly in your search for personal fulfillment.

▲ Peridot is a gemstone of compassion, health, and abundance.

You are capable of having strong feelings, but it can be hard for you to show them, as you prefer to make decisions based on reason, and may find it difficult to trust your intuition. Virgoans have pure motives, but you sometimes get so caught up with your sense of duty and need to serve that you sacrifice important ambitions, and later regret having let opportunities pass you by.

You are surprisingly romantic, and can be quite uncompromising in your quest for real love, often saving yourself until the right person comes along.

DRESS SENSE

Some Virgoans are extremely unkempt, but most of you are immaculately groomed, and you take great care with your appearance. Whatever it is you are wearing, the overall effect is usually very neat and tidy. You avoid loose-fitting, baggy garments, choosing smart, functional outfits that will last. Virgoans are sensible, and you are prepared to shop around for a bargain, rather than risk the chance of overspending. When it comes to matters of style, modesty and caution prevail, and you generally opt for fairly conventional trends.

Women tend to favor wearing blouses and skirts for work, often with greens, browns, and grays. Accessories will be tidy and shoes are always freshly polished. You may take some time putting the finishing touches to your image, and then make readjustments as the day progresses. For leisure, you love relaxing in natural fibers, and have a weakness for a pretty dress. You also like to wear pants, but never give a sloppy impression.

Men feel efficient and comfortable in a suit, and you can be quite meticulous about positioning your tie. White shirts are favored, and are changed every day without fail. Clean clothes make you think more clearly, while dirty ones put you in a bad mood. For leisure, you prefer crisp sweatsuits and understated casuals. On rare occasions, you are quite experimental when dressing up.

HEALTH

VIRGOANS usually take a very active interest in their own bodies, and you are sensible enough to stay in tiptop condition for the most part. Your sometimes-delicate constitution benefits from such foresight, and provided you maintain a balanced approach and don't become too obsessive, you should enjoy good health for a good many years.

Worrying can make you prone to hypochondria, however, and small symptoms are often blown out of proportion. A Virgoan's nervous system is very sensitive, and you find it hard to stay calm.

When genuine illness strikes, no matter how it affects you, you do everything within your power to fight it. You work hard to regain perfect health, sometimes taking extreme measures and persisting until recovery is absolute.

The main parts of the body connected to Virgo are the digestive tract and the skin. When worried and uptight, you may become susceptible to irritable bowel syndrome and/or eczema-like complaints. Although eating the right foods can help, staying relaxed is much more effective in combatting these conditions.

▲ This detail showing the sign of Virgo features in a well-preserved fifth-century mosaic at Maltezana on the Greek island of Astypalea.

LIFESTYLE CHOICES

Many Virgoans like to have modern homes, as these are much easier to run and clean. You prefer simple buildings, and do not like to live in anything too showy. You can find city life pretentious, and feel a lot more relaxed in a rural setting. However, modern careers mean this is not always possible, and you may have to settle for living within striking distance of the country. Virgoans have a taste for wood and other natural materials. Stripped floors and tiles are popular, and you have a preference for large rugs and drapes that can be easily moved around. You usually choose carpets that are highly practical and durable.

For decor, you like to create a bright atmosphere, and light colors are prevalent. Both sexes have home maintenance skills that you use to achieve a functional, cheerful design throughout your home, which is both welcoming and relaxing.

Some Virgoans have a tendency to be overly fussy, and you may fill your homes with lots of ornaments and knickknacks, or grand displays of china that are cleaned regularly, but never used. You love to have a sense of order, but can get carried away!

Virgoans are cautious and thrifty when it comes to spending cash. Even for minor purchases, you are liable to research them thoroughly to make sure that you get the best bargain. You don't see the point of shelling out money without good reason, and can be quite humble in your tastes.

EXERCISE

IN TERMS OF health, Virgoans generally like to be in good shape, and you are usually motivated to exercise on a regular basis. Being outside in the fresh air does wonders for your whole system, and cycling (right), walking, and running are the most popular ways of keeping fit.

When exercising indoors, you tend to like dance lessons and aerobics classes and, as with all sports you take part in, you work hard on perfecting your technique.

Virgoans can be very restless physically, and may suffer from nervous tension. Because of this, learning to be calm both in body and mind brings tangible and lasting rewards. Many Virgoans find meditation an effective way to relieve stress.

Your attention to detail makes keeping track of finances simple, and you are unlikely to have debts. A few disorganized Virgoans do have chaotic, messy finances, but most of you are very careful, taking great comfort in knowing how even the smallest amount was spent. You provide for the future without really trying, as your modest lifestyle means that you usually live on much less than you earn.

Long-term security is important to a Virgoan, and you are generally very interested in investing your money somehow. Slow, steady profits appeal to you, although sometimes you can be too cautious for your own good.

VIRGOANS AT PLAY

Virgoans are versatile, and keep busy with hobbies. These have every chance of developing into a viable business, although your desire for perfection can mean that you never believe your products are good enough to sell! Virgoans really like to keep busy, and your leisure hours will usually find you engaged in some sort of fruitful activity. With your desire to help humanity, being involved in charity work is very fulfilling and a good way to make contact with like-minded others.

Virgoans have sharp, lively brains, which you use to focus on one or two specialized interests. Whether academic or practical, these may develop into rewarding hobbies, and you can become a real expert in your field. You are skilled with crafts that require careful attention, such as needlepoint and model-making.

Gardening is popular, and it is also a very good way for you to unwind. Virgoans are keen students, and you are often found at evening classes. You see your friends regularly, and really appreciate doing a variety of things with them. When they come to dinner, you are likely to prepare your latest health food recipe.

Virgoans don't like it when they feel as though life is becoming disorganized and unmanageable. You want to know precisely what needs to be done, and love making lists to clarify tasks. You can be very picky, and become quite upset if others fail to live up to your exacting standards.

Being bored makes you fidgety, and you try always to keep busy. You find irresponsible and immodest behavior really annoying, and have little time for those who make a habit of saying one thing and doing another. For a Virgoan, humility and consistency are very important.

THE PERFECT LOVE MATCH

Discover how Virgoans fare in relationships with other star signs

Aries	Inconsiderate	❤❤
Taurus	Lasting joy	❤❤❤❤❤
Gemini	Surprise hit	❤❤❤❤
Cancer	Caring partner	❤❤❤❤
Leo	Absolutely not!	❤
Virgo	Pragmatic soul mates	❤❤❤❤❤
Libra	Too impractical	❤❤❤
Scorpio	Good, but intense	❤❤❤❤
Sagittarius	Restless mismatch	❤❤
Capricorn	Everyone's a winner	❤❤❤❤❤
Aquarius	Keep walking!	❤
Pisces	Compassionate love	❤❤❤

LIBRA SEPTEMBER 23–OCTOBER 22

The sign of Libra is ruled by the scales. You are thoughtful and sensitive, and seek balance and harmony whenever possible. Librans need people more than other signs, and sometimes find it difficult to be alone; good relationships with others are the key to your happiness and security. Intellectual and refined, you think very carefully before making decisions, preferring to weigh all the pros and cons of any situation before taking action. Sometimes you even prefer to sit on the fence rather than commit yourself to one side.

You enjoy discussions and arguments, and will often take the opposing view to make a conversation more interesting—much to the infuriation of those around you!

You are also diplomatic and charming, with a real gift for being able to listen and sympathize. This ability to communicate well makes you very sociable, and you usually have lots of friends. However, you can be a bit of a people pleaser, and may compromise yourself in the process.

Librans dislike creating waves and, as a result, you often store up problems rather than face any form of unpleasantness.

▲ Libra is associated with the Justice card in tarot, which represents balance, reasonableness, a good sense of judgment, and fairness.

▶ Entitled Libra, Signs of the Zodiac, this rendition of Libran scales appeared in a 15th-century **Atlas Celeste** (Star Atlas). The artist is unknown.

TRADITIONAL ASSOCIATIONS

Librans are most closely associated with the following:

COLORS:	Pale blue, pink
COUNTRIES:	China, Austria
TAROT CARD:	Number 8, Justice
FLOWERS:	Mallow
BIRTHSTONE:	Sapphire, emerald
ANIMALS:	Swans
OCCUPATIONS:	Counselor, musician, lawyer, psychologist
HERBS:	Aloe
TREES:	White sycamore, fig
CITIES:	Frankfurt, Vienna, Copenhagen, Arles
FOOD:	Milk, honey, fruit

But occasionally you can benefit from confronting issues head-on. You present an image of calm to the outside world, but this laid-backness masks how much you are affected by what goes on around you.

Librans are highly principled, and your strong morals and concern for fair play mean that you become upset by any perceived injustice. You try to live up to your ideals, and you sometimes miss opportunities because you want to be certain that you have made the right decision. Once you have learned to trust and act on your instincts, you become a doer as well as a thinker.

THE LIBRAN MAN

The typical Libran man has a pleasing face, which maintains a serene expression even when upset or angry. Your bone structure is usually quite delicate, and your hair very fine. You walk with graceful and thoughtful steps, and are conscious of your appearance, grooming yourself carefully before going out.

Librans are blessed with abundant social skills, and your wit and charm ensure popularity. You love exploring ideas and concepts, and really enjoy lively conversations with others. You usually have plenty of advice to give, but aren't always so good at practicing what you preach!

Libran men have a strong feminine side, and therefore relate easily to the opposite sex from an early age. You are artistic, and appreciate many forms of beauty; in fact, your love for the finer things in life can make you quite indulgent in your pursuit of pleasure. You are prone to laziness, which should not be left unchecked.

A strong partnership is vital for you to feel complete. You have a great need for intimacy, and a loving relationship brings you deep and lasting fulfillment.

THE LIBRAN WOMAN

Libran women have well-proportioned and generally attractive features. You tend to be slim, with a curvy figure and fairly broad hips. Like Libran men, your face displays serenity and poise even in times of crisis, and you move with elegance and grace. You are very aware of how you look, and like to check mirrors for reassurance.

You possess an excellent mind, and are more than capable of holding your own in sharp debates. You are at your best when working with others, however, as occasionally you require a second opinion to make a decision. Librans are very tactful, and people find it easy to trust you and relax in your company.

Your gentle, subtle manner disguises a fierce determination—the original "steel magnolia!" When necessary, you can be really tough and forthright in achieving your aims. You crave creature comforts, and may find it hard to do without. Libran women usually require beauty and tranquillity before they can really relax and unwind. You are very romantic, and have a tremendous amount of love and energy to put into a relationship. You do not enjoy being alone, and if single, you will actively seek a partner. Of all the signs of the zodiac, Librans truly find themselves through others.

▲ Character traits associated with the mallow flower include a sweet disposition and beneficence.

▲ Sapphires are said to symbolize creative expression, intuition, and hope.

DRESS SENSE

Librans are very image-conscious, and are concerned about wearing the right clothes. You can take a lot of time preparing to go out, and you will often try on different outfits and then change your mind at the last minute! Some Librans become obsessed with preening and dressing themselves, and can be quite narcissistic.

Most of you have good taste, and coordinate outfits harmoniously, usually avoiding clashes of style and color. Romantic looks are favored by both sexes, and you are happy to spend money to keep your wardrobe well stocked. Fashionable clothes usually look good on you, provided they are not too hard and aggressive, as you prefer soft textures and tones that subtly enhance your attractiveness and presence.

At work, women are at their best in slightly formal styles. If you choose something too casual, the overall effect may be inappropriate. When dressing up, Libran women look stunning wearing flowing dresses in pastel shades. You like to add a splash of individuality with accessories, and fragrant perfumes complement your romantic mood. Even in jeans and casuals, female Librans look very feminine.

Male Librans can be quite fashionable in their choice of work clothes, selecting suits with real pizzazz. Although for some casual wear you can be surprisingly unfussy, you will always dress up for an important date since romance is something you take very seriously indeed!

LIFESTYLE CHOICES

Librans hate noise and clutter, and your well-developed aesthetic sense means that you are adversely affected by harsh and unattractive environments. If possible, you prefer to live in a beautiful area, but you

HEALTH

LIBRANS stay healthy provided they keep their body well balanced. However, you can find it hard to resist indulgent living. Too many late nights and constant rich foods mean that you will become run down easily, and if you do not take remedial action, illness may result. Be kind to your system, and most minor ailments simply disappear.

The kidneys and liver are the main body areas related to the sign of Libra. Your sensitive body can become stressed quite easily. When this happens, these vital organs may not function at their normal efficiency, and you may experience a buildup of toxins, resulting in headaches and chronic tiredness. Most of these symptoms will be alleviated by taking it easy and eating light foods that don't place a strain on your digestive system. When your energy levels recover, light exercise is advisable.

As some Librans are prone to a sluggish metabolism, keeping to a moderate diet is very important. If you do become ill, beautiful surroundings and plenty of attention from friends is guaranteed to aid the healing process; being isolated can only make you more susceptible to disease.

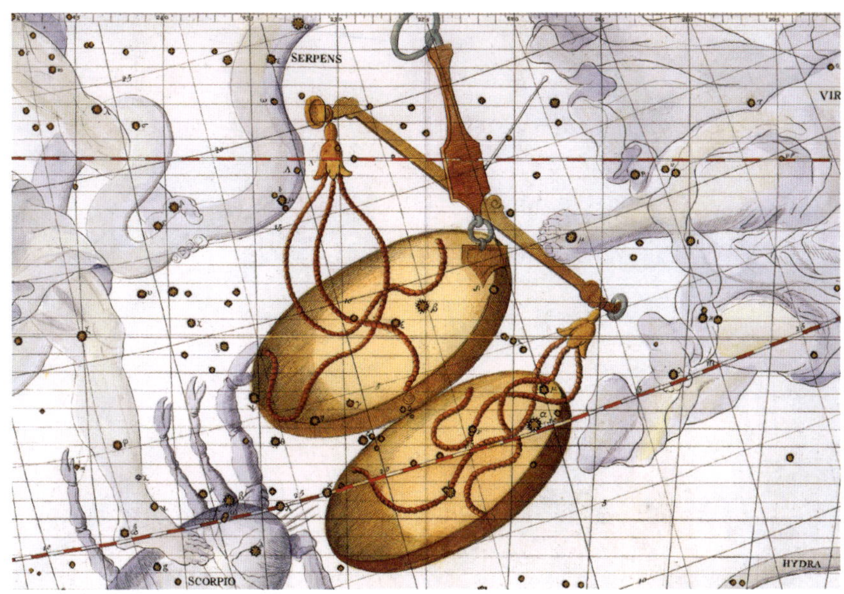

▲ An engraving of the constellation of Libra from John Flamsteed's **Atlas Coelestis**, published in 1729, hand-colored by the artist, James Thornhill.

will do your utmost to make wherever you call home tranquil and harmonious.

You are skilled at creating an atmosphere that is gently relaxing, using soft furnishings and warm designs to create a feeling of peace and comfort. Librans like balance in their homes, and will try to arrange the furniture in every room to achieve a sense of proportion and space. You also experiment with lighting, using dimmer switches, candles, and spotlights to set the desired mood.

Because clutter grates on your nerves, you will tidy up and do the household chores on a regular basis, although you may hire help if you can afford it. You use your natural good taste to beautify your home, and make it an enjoyable and special place for others to visit. Being able to offer hospitality is very important, as you won't be happy if you are always stuck at home alone. Living in a remote area is unlikely to appeal to you, as you need to feel that you are accessible to your friends.

Librans like to maintain a good standard of living, and may find it difficult to economize. This can result in overdrafts and large credit-card debts before you realize the seriousness of the situation and finally take action to put things right. You are resourceful and earn money with ease, but you may experience problems as a result of your somewhat relaxed attitude toward money management—a little prudence and self-control will do much to ensure your continued prosperity.

EXERCISE

YOU can be quite lazy when it comes to exercising regularly, and any fitness routine must be fun in order to sustain your interest for any length of time. Librans especially dislike being uncomfortable, and are not suited to punishing fitness programs.

Many Librans take up martial arts, such as t'ai chi (right), as you appreciate the concept of yin and yang, with its emphasis on the balance of body and mind. Walking, swimming, and dancing are also popular activities, and you find them far more enjoyable when done with friends or as part of a class. As you desire always to look good, think about joining a health club—you enjoy pampering yourself, and your vanity is a powerful spur to getting fit and staying in shape.

You enjoy spending money on luxuries, and are very generous to friends and family members. You can be easily swayed by a hard-luck story, however, and should be wary of those who try to take advantage of your kindness.

Librans will cheerfully work with diligence to fund their preferred lifestyle, but learning the details of various investment plans may bore you to tears. If you find it difficult to make decisions about your future financial plans, seeking professional advice is strongly recommended.

Joint business ventures with friends can work out well, particularly if they are based on a genuine interest rather than just a whim. You enjoy shared responsibility, as your motivation is generally much stronger when others are involved.

LIBRANS AT PLAY

Librans are very sociable and prefer to spend their leisure time with others, so rather than doing something on your own, you usually invite a friend along. Art exhibitions, movies, nightclubs, and concerts are your favorite ways to socialize. You love discussing what you have seen and done by relaxing over dinner with friends.

Many Librans are very musical, and as well as attending performances, you may play an instrument yourself. Your CD or album collection is likely to be large, as listening to music is a favorite way for you to unwind. You prefer harmonious tunes that create a tranquil atmosphere.

Librans have a gentle creativity that can be hard to express in words. Photography and painting may attract you, as you are drawn toward capturing images of beauty. Once you have found something that you really like, you study it seriously, and it may develop into a lifelong hobby or career.

Librans are quite inclined to laziness, and periodically take a complete break from any form of activity to recharge your batteries. You enjoy verbal banter, and are frustrated if someone always agrees with you. You can have quite a lot of stored aggression, and arguing provides a positive channel for its release. Librans need plenty of time to reach a decision, and being forced to make up your mind before you are ready makes you feel quite stressed. You love easygoing environments that allow you to really relax. Librans need attention, but generally avoid the spotlight. Lack of human contact can lead to depression and for happiness, nothing beats warm, solid friendships.

THE PERFECT LOVE MATCH

Discover how Librans fare in relationships with other star signs

Aries	Perfect blend	❤❤❤❤❤
Taurus	Every so often	❤❤❤
Gemini	Smashing!	❤❤❤❤❤
Cancer	Unlikely	❤❤
Leo	Plenty of passion	❤❤❤❤
Virgo	Overly practical	❤❤❤
Libra	Balanced love	❤❤❤❤
Scorpio	Too much!	❤
Sagittarius	Yes!	❤❤❤❤❤
Capricorn	Definitely not	❤
Aquarius	Double air sign delight	❤❤❤❤❤
Pisces	Possibilities	❤❤❤

SCORPIO OCTOBER 23–NOVEMBER 21

The depth and intensity of your emotions give you an inner power that demands instant expression. Scorpios are creatures of passion, and your focused desires help you to achieve your aims. Mysterious and fearless, you are willing to undergo total transformation when necessary, rising like the phoenix to claim new life. Scorpios have a penetrating insight, always seeking what lies beneath the surface. You can be ruthlessly self-critical in your quest for truth, understanding only too well what makes you tick.

Your perceptive mind enjoys investigating all aspects of human nature, including many that are taboo. The resulting awareness of your own motivations produces a healthy suspicion of other people, and sometimes you take this to extremes, becoming very reluctant to trust anyone.

You have an excellent memory for how things have affected you on an emotional level. Scorpios have an inherent sense of justice and loyalty and your fixed nature means that you hold onto hurts and betrayals for a long time. Deep-seated bitterness may make it hard to dispel

▲ Scorpio is associated with the Death card in tarot, which can signify a transformation of some kind, progress, and spiritual rebirth.

▶ Detail from "Scorpio" as depicted in **Urania's Mirror**, a set of 32 constellation cards engraved by Sidney Hall and published in London ca 1825.

Antares
Lesath

TRADITIONAL ASSOCIATIONS

Scorpios are most closely associated with the following:

COLORS:	Dark red, black
COUNTRIES:	Tibet, Morocco, Norway
TAROT CARD:	Number 13, Death
FLOWERS:	Amaryllis
BIRTHSTONE:	Opal, turquoise
ANIMALS:	Scorpions, eagles, lizards
OCCUPATIONS:	Doctor, banker, pharmacist, financial analyst
HERBS:	Witch hazel
TREES:	Blackthorn, birch
CITIES:	Cincinnati, Fez, Washington, D.C.
FOOD:	Meat and spicy foods

vengeful thoughts, and you are patient and secretive when plotting revenge.

Scorpios are uncompromising, and when a commitment is made, you stick to it. You need to feel good about what you are doing, and clear goals are very important, because you hate feeling as if you are in limbo. Emotional fulfillment is absolutely vital, and if you don't have it in one area, you will seek it in another. Scorpios have a charismatic, magnetic presence that usually attracts the attention of others. Your deep sexuality provides the source of your tremendous energy. Whether you use this creative force for good or evil is a moral dilemma that only you can solve.

THE SCORPIO MAN

The typical Scorpio man has strong features with penetrating, hypnotic eyes. Your body hair is likely to be thick and abundant, and your heavy eyebrows often meet in the middle. You walk with confident, purposeful steps, and usually have a broad, well-muscled chest. Your sex appeal is usually obvious, and many women find it hard not to steal a glance as you pass by.

You have strong opinions, and plunge yourself into life with abandon. Scorpios are fearlessly honest, and this can sometimes compel you to confront others with the truth. You are master of your own destiny and react violently to unwelcome interference. You like to explore the full range of human desire, including the darker sides!

Scorpios have the potential to transform their nature, and you will probably go through two or three complete life changes, each time emerging wiser and more whole.

These periods can be very testing, but they are a necessary part of your evolution. The reward for undergoing such trials is a real sense of peace and freedom, something you instinctively seek. You love sharing your intense emotions in a relationship, and need a woman who can handle your powerful blend of passion and control.

THE SCORPIO WOMAN

The typical Scorpio woman is sultry, and well aware of her sex appeal. You have magnetic eyes that command attention, with a body that is curvy and strong. You have a tangible physical presence. Scorpios have a sixth sense and an ability to read minds, which some may find unnerving.

Scorpio women exude confidence and control. Inside you may be a torrent of emotion, but you are careful not to let down your guard. Both thoughtful and intuitive, you are interested in the deeper issues of life, having little time for shallow beliefs and superficial behavior. You take full responsibility for your actions, and answer to no one.

▲ Among the characteristics embodied by the amaryllis flower are pride and determination.

▲ Turquoise is associated with clear and honest lines of communication.

You have many passions and talents, and it can be difficult to decide which to focus on. Once your goals are set, you persevere with remarkable spirit and conviction until success is achieved.

Scorpio women are tough and resilient, yet also extremely feminine. This combination sets you apart, and makes you very choosy when it comes to relationships. You are naturally dominant and assertive, liking to stay in control of your feelings. With the right man, however, you have the courage to express your deepest self.

DRESS SENSE

Scorpios like to wear clothes that emphasize your natural magnetism, and you can be quite bold with your image. You are comfortable with your sexuality, and not afraid to show it. Dark colors are favored, and these give you an air of mystery and allure. In your quest to look good, you are prepared to spend money on quality items, but would rather go without than buy something that you are not completely taken by. You follow your own rules where trends are concerned, but are unlikely to stray too far from conventional styles.

Scorpio women enjoy looking glamorous and sexy. If it is important to project a powerful image at work, you will dress effectively, and are not averse to using your looks to your advantage. When you want to relax, your choice of clothes depends on your mood—one day you may wear loose-fitting casuals, and the next, skintight leather trousers with a revealing top. For a really hot date you always dress imaginatively, with confidence, daring, and flamboyance, using makeup and perfume to add a splash of magic.

For work, men prefer well-cut suits, and if you can afford it, these will be the best designer labels. In your leisure hours, you enjoy wearing manly casuals; when you really want to impress the opposite sex, you choose stylish clothes that maximize your charisma.

LIFESTYLE CHOICES

Privacy is important to a Scorpio, and you need to have a home where you can unwind and not be disturbed. You are fond of old buildings with character, and are

HEALTH

Scorpios have a great deal of stamina and a highly resilient constitution, which means that your general health is usually good. You tend to take this for granted, however, and can push yourself to the absolute limit with excessive work and play. Your vital force is strong, but it needs to be respected at all times.

Some of the illness you experience may be psychosomatic in origin, relating to blocked energy in your life. If this happens, you should try and recognize what is happening, and then act accordingly. Scorpios are prone to nervous tension, and this can affect muscles in the shoulders, neck, and back. All of these respond well to massage and total relaxation, both of which are highly recommended.

The main parts of the body related to the sign of Scorpio are the reproductive organs, the bladder, and the large intestine. It's very important for you to eliminate toxins from your body every so often. It could be a worthwhile exercise to seek advice from a nutritionist and periodically embark on a short, cleansing diet. If adhered to correctly, such diets are very conducive to maintaining optimum health levels in the longer term.

▲ A detail showing the house of Scorpio in Prince Iskandar's horoscope, which features in **The Book of the Birth of Iskandar**, dated 1411.

quite sensitive to atmosphere. A prospective house or apartment has to have the right "feel" before you will commit to it.

Some Scorpios prefer to live in the country, and you are also very attracted to water. Your stormy nature finds solace near rivers and lakes. However, as most of you like to have plenty going on around you, only a city will do for the majority.

Scorpios have very distinctive ideas about decorating and furnishing their homes. Strong, vibrant color schemes with predominant dark tones are popular. You love plush sofas and chairs, with rich fabrics such as silk, velvet, and satin for curtains and drapes. The overall effect is often exotic and intense, and you enjoy spending time creating something special.

Scorpios don't like too much bare space, and instead of having vast expanses of blank walls, you prefer to hang tasteful pictures and photographs. When entertaining, you use lights and mirrors to help vary the mood, and to create a feeling of intimacy for your guests.

Scorpios have a need for self-preservation, and are very careful with finances. Even when circumstances are difficult, you always seem to get by. Your intuition finds plenty of ways to make money, and you possess a strong desire to be rich. Sometimes you are very jealous of others, and forget to count your blessings; but usually you will work extremely hard in order to achieve success. Scorpios really enjoy spending, and love the power that

EXERCISE

INSUFFICIENT exercise will leave many a Scorpio feeling emotionally out of balance. So intense are Scorpios in nature, that they need to take on demanding physical challenges, such as endurance running.

The martial arts—karate, judo, kick-boxing—and other tough sports give a positive outlet for potentially dangerous levels of aggression. At a considerably gentler level, aerobics, jogging (right), and working out in a gym help to release pent-up tension, while helping to tone your body.

You are also attracted to water sports of all kinds, but especially to swimming and scuba diving. Scorpios love going down into the depths of the ocean to discover a completely different dimension of experience.

wealth provides. Once you are secure and settled, you can be extremely generous.

Although you like to keep quite a tight control of your finances, you have a good nose for a successful investment. Before making any decisions, you investigate various options in depth, and then make commitments. You are prepared to take considerable risks, and on occasion display an inherent killer instinct.

Many of you consider running a business or being self-employed. A born survivor, you are able to transform and adapt when others would go under. Scorpios are competitive, and you thrive in the dog-eat-dog environment of modern trade. Answering only to yourself is very appealing, and psychologically, you have much to gain from being in charge of your own livelihood.

SCORPIOS AT PLAY

Leisure time is very precious to you, and not a moment of it gets wasted! Many Scorpios actively pursue pleasure, and your social life is usually tremendously rich and varied. Bars, nightclubs, and lively parties make you feel really alive. You get a serious buzz from intense and exciting environments.

Scorpios enjoy having a few close friends who have different interests, and getting together with them is your favorite way to unwind after a stressful day. You appreciate good food and drink, especially when shared with others, and you may become absorbed in studying wine as a hobby. You have a reflective and imaginative side that is drawn to reading and watching movies.

Scorpios love anything to do with crime detection, mystery, and the occult, so books and movies on these topics are fascinating to you. Occasionally, you need to be still and silent, as serious moods give you an urge to be on your own. Periods of inner communion are very necessary for your well-being.

Scorpios like to keep their thoughts private, and you are very uncomfortable in situations that force you to reveal personal, intimate information. But you have no qualms about probing the hidden secrets of others, and relish the chance to ask leading questions.

Your emotions are powerful, and you enjoy feeling that they are under control. Many Scorpios get depressed without action, and need to live at a pace that is emotionally charged.

THE PERFECT LOVE MATCH

Discover how Scorpios fare in relationships with other star signs

Sign	Match	Rating
Aries	Passionate fling	♥♥♥
Taurus	Winning attraction	♥♥♥♥
Gemini	Forget it!	♥
Cancer	Water sign perfection	♥♥♥♥♥
Leo	Very good or very bad	♥♥♥
Virgo	Easygoing love	♥♥♥♥
Libra	Uncommitted	♥
Scorpio	Right on!	♥♥♥♥
Sagittarius	Fun affair	♥♥♥
Capricorn	Rock-solid romance	♥♥♥♥♥
Aquarius	Sometimes lasts	♥♥♥
Pisces	Deep	♥♥♥♥

SAGITTARIUS NOVEMBER 22–DECEMBER 21

Sagittarians are both restless and visionary, and love to explore new horizons. You have a bold and optimistic attitude, and treat life as a journey full of adventure. Your positive outlook often attracts good fortune. Whatever you encounter along the way is greeted with a warm heart, an open mind, and a ready smile. Sagittarians have an expansive nature that needs to reach out and discover new challenges. This can be on a mental level, as a student thirsty for fresh knowledge, or on a physical level, with a strong passion for travel.

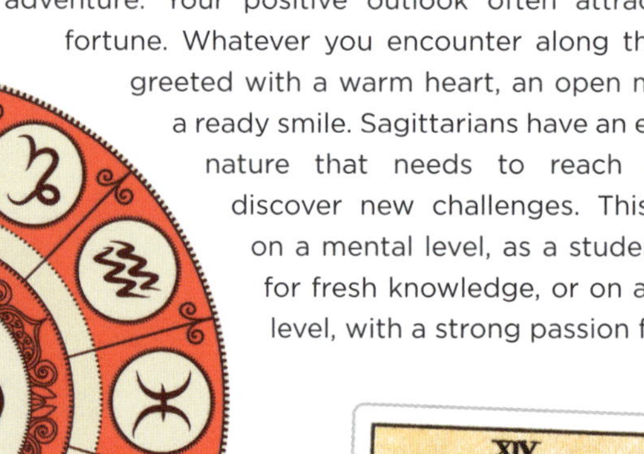

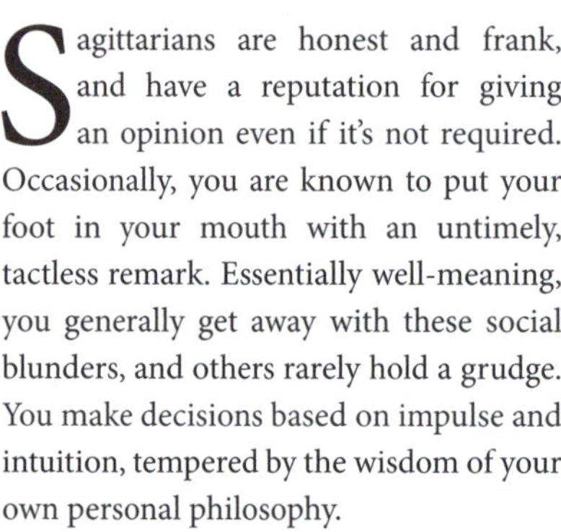

Sagittarians are honest and frank, and have a reputation for giving an opinion even if it's not required. Occasionally, you are known to put your foot in your mouth with an untimely, tactless remark. Essentially well-meaning, you generally get away with these social blunders, and others rarely hold a grudge. You make decisions based on impulse and intuition, tempered by the wisdom of your own personal philosophy.

Sagittarians tend to take risks, and you love stretching yourself by jumping into the unknown—although sometimes you fall flat on your face! However, you usually

▲ Sagittarius is associated with Temperance in tarot, which represents patience, frugality, and a harmony between material and spiritual things.

► An illustration of the constellation Sagittarius, from Cicero's **Aratus**, published in the 11th century and held at the British Library, London.

SAGITTARIUS

TRADITIONAL ASSOCIATIONS

Sagittarians are most closely associated with the following:

COLORS:	Purple, dark blues
COUNTRIES:	Australia, Spain
TAROT CARD:	Number 14, Temperance
FLOWERS:	Dandelions
BIRTHSTONE:	Topaz, amethyst
ANIMALS:	Horses, stags, peacocks
OCCUPATIONS:	Travel representative, teacher, lawyer, veterinarian
HERBS:	Borage
TREES:	Oak, lime, mulberry
CITIES:	Sydney, Avignon, Stuttgart, Toronto
FOOD:	Food from around the world

land on your feet, and quickly bounce back from any mistakes.

Most Sagittarians are idealistic, with a keen interest in the culture and beliefs of other countries. You ask probing questions about morality and social issues, sometimes developing passionate convictions. When this happens, however, you must watch a tendency to preach blindly to everyone in sight.

Sagittarians like movement, and if you feel that your life is stagnating you soon become bored and start looking around for a way to escape. Ultimately, your spirit longs to be free.

THE SAGITTARIAN MAN

Sagittarian men usually have tall, athletic bodies, and no matter what your height, your thighs are sturdy. You walk with wide strides, frequently swinging your arms. Your eyes are full of vitality and usually have a slight hint of mischief. You have a humorous expression, and your whole face lights up whenever you laugh.

You are at heart a bit of a gambler, and occasionally can be quite reckless. This wild side sometimes causes you to throw caution to the wind in order to test your inner strengths. You enjoy being physical, and are attracted to the great outdoors. Confined spaces can quickly bring on feelings of claustrophobia, and will suffocate your basic lively nature.

Your restlessness and desire to seek new challenges mean it may be some time, if ever, before you are really ready to settle down. Sagittarians have to struggle to keep commitments; otherwise, there is a danger of having too superficial a lifestyle.

You possess a great sense of humor, and are always glad to share a joke with others. Bold and confident, your extrovert approach is inspiring, too. For you, fulfillment is reached through acting on your instincts. Sagittarian men are romantic, and love the companionship of women.

THE SAGITTARIAN WOMAN

The Sagittarian woman has a striking face, often with handsome features. Your body is lithe, and, like the men, your thighs are well developed. Your eyes are bright, and your expression is frank and honest. You have a hearty appearance and walk with confident, uninhibited steps, looking directly ahead.

Strong and independent, Sagittarian women are the gypsies of the zodiac. You feel compelled to follow your passions, and can roam far and wide in your search for happiness. Wherever you decide to call home, freedom of expression is always important, and you rebel against the constraints of convention. Sagittarians think for themselves, and you are always ruled by your own moral code.

▲ Considered the most mighty of all trees, the oak stands for courage, strength, and power.

▲ Amethyst is said to counterbalance an addictive personality.

You are very honest, and wear your heart on your sleeve. This openness gives you a certain vulnerability but it is also your greatest asset. After a few hard knocks, you learn to take care and avoid real trouble.

Relationships are one area where you must be careful, as your extreme optimism and impulsiveness can result in disappointment. You are a powerful woman, and need a self-assured partner who makes you feel both loved and free.

DRESS SENSE

Sagittarians are attracted to casual, unrestrictive clothes. It can be quite an ordeal stuffing yourself into formal attire, and you avoid this whenever possible. You faithfully stick to trusted items, often grabbing the first thing that comes to hand. The result is a slightly carefree image, for you rarely spend time on careful grooming.

Many Sagittarians put off buying new clothes until it is absolutely necessary—and when you finally do so, your purchases are usually hasty and impulsive, with only a cursory search for a bargain. These shopping expeditions often result in mistakes and some garments may have to be exchanged.

Female Sagittarians are attracted to country styles that reflect their preference for an outdoor life. If forced to dress up for work, you prefer to wear interesting colors. For relaxing, you enjoy the comfort of sweatsuits, and these often become like a second skin. A romantic evening gives you a chance to show your bohemian soul, and you respond by dressing exotically.

Sagittarian men will often wear a loud, colorful tie when confined in a suit. This twist of humor is typical. Leisure wear is usually sporty, and you favor generously cut casuals that have a free, easy feel. For a really big date, you are prepared to change your style and submit to formal clothes.

LIFESTYLE CHOICES

Sagittarians have a strong affinity for the country, and many of you tend to make your homes there. You simply love wide-open spaces and the freedom of the wilderness. City life with all its pollution, noise, and intense population can be

HEALTH

Sagittarians have active, physical lifestyles that keep them robust and healthy. You like to move around and use your body, and this precludes most minor ills from affecting you. On the rare occasions when you do fall ill, you concentrate intensely on getting well, as you find being a patient incredibly dull. Such a tendency usually means a quick recovery, and you display a cheerful optimism even when in pain.

The parts of the body connected to your sign include the liver, hips, and thighs. A weakness for rich foods and wines may lead to plumpness, especially in middle age. To get rid of these fatty areas, vigorous activity must be combined with a sensible diet. You have a very indulgent streak that can tax your liver's ability to cope.

In later years, arthritis and rheumatism can affect your hips. Modest exercise offers some protection, as does avoiding prolonged exposure to damp. Sagittarians can be clumsy, resulting in various bumps and bruises.

Experience will teach you to be extra careful when rushing around. Your love for reckless sports also provides potential for serious accidents. Although lucky, you would be wise not to push your luck too far.

stifling. If you do live in an urban environment, you are often forced to go for a drive just to keep your sanity.

Any apartment or house, no matter what its location, must have a feeling of space, light, and air, with plenty of room to breathe. You find small, stuffy apartments depressing, and will gladly spend extra money to secure the right place. Sagittarians like simple, no-nonsense furniture and basic curtains and rugs. You are not inclined toward fancy interior designs, and prefer one or two very simple colors as decoration.

Sagittarians, not known for their tidiness, prefer to relax at home without worrying about making a mess. Artifacts from different cultures may be scattered about, revealing your love for travel. You are very sociable, and an affable host. Friends are always invited to stay.

▲ Detail from "Sagittarius" as depicted in **Urania's Mirror**, a set of 32 constellation cards engraved by Sidney Hall and published in London ca 1825.

Sagittarians are by nature extravagant, and you may find that despite your best intentions, money slips through your fingers. You have little desire to scrutinize your finances, and your impulsive approach can mean that sometimes debts are incurred at a rather alarming rate. But hope springs eternal, and you always believe that more funds will arrive, even if there is nothing on the horizon. However, you generally work hard, though, and put in enough overtime to balance the books.

Sagittarians are very generous, and happily share their wealth—occasionally with people who take advantage. You hate

EXERCISE

WHEN it comes to taking regular exercise, Sagittarians greatly enjoy team sports. Volleyball (right), football, baseball, hockey, wrestling, and basketball are all perennial favorites, whereas quieter pursuits such as golf or bowling may strike you as being a little too tame.

Above all, you need to feel as if you've had a good workout and a team sport is most likely to achieve this. There is also something in you that likes the sensation of taking part in a physical competition.

Sagittarians also love hiking and camping in the mountains, taking in wild scenery, and breathing in plenty of fresh air. If you are seeking something more exciting, try skiing, snow boarding, or surfing.

being miserly, and feel sorry for those who are. Inside every Sagittarian is a potential gambler. This may never surface, but if it does, you could develop an addiction to racing, casinos, or others forms of betting.

When it comes to investing, you find wild speculation very attractive, and more than one Sagittarian has gotten burned this way. In the right environment, your gambling instincts are very assured, especially in conjunction with expert tips. You need a slight sense of risk and adventure, finding things such as safe pensions and saving plans rather boring. Sagittarians are generally lucky, and have a way of stumbling into money.

SAGITTARIANS AT PLAY

Sagittarians like to make full use of all available leisure time. You have plenty of energy for work and play, preferring to have at least a few evening activities planned each week. Natural students, you jump at the chance to branch out into new fields of knowledge, and can be very disciplined when you discover a subject that really fires your imagination. Favored topics are languages, religions, anthropology, sociology, and philosophy.

A gregarious party animal, you also certainly know how to relax and have fun! Your friendliness has the effect of putting those around you at ease, and most Sagittarians have a large circle of friends. You can be quite bawdy after a couple of drinks, and keep everyone amused with your jokes and tall stories!

You love animals, and keeping pets is a rewarding and challenging hobby. Sagittarians are always very drawn to travel, and for some, this wanderlust leads to long sojourns abroad, while others satisfy their appetite with exotic vacations and trips. You love exploring diverse cultures and sampling the various tastes and sensations from your many travels around the world.

You need variety, freedom, and movement, finding dead-end situations heavy and oppressive. Sagittarians like to be honest and open at all times, and being forced to keep your feelings hidden is a real strain. You do not hold onto the past, preferring instead to look forward with optimism and hope.

Every once in a while you enjoy a spending binge of some sort, as you hate having to be careful with money. Sagittarians need to take risks, or otherwise, your energy stagnates.

THE PERFECT LOVE MATCH

Discover how Sagittarians fare in relationships with other star signs

Sign	Match	Rating
Aries	Love perfection	❤❤❤❤❤
Taurus	Hidden flaws	❤
Gemini	Strong attraction	❤❤❤❤
Cancer	Once in a blue moon	❤❤
Leo	Feel the heat!	❤❤❤❤❤
Virgo	Real clash	❤❤
Libra	Sweet and lasting	❤❤❤❤❤
Scorpio	Short-term sizzler!	❤❤❤
Sagittarius	Gypsy passion	❤❤❤❤❤
Capricorn	No!	❤
Aquarius	Yes!	❤❤❤❤❤
Pisces	Sexy affair	❤❤❤

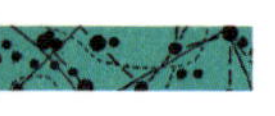

CAPRICORN DECEMBER 22–JANUARY 19

Capricorns are ambitious, with an instinctual drive to reach the top. The route is carefully planned, and you work steadily to fulfill your personal goals. You are sure-footed, and cling to your vision with tenacity and drive. Once the dizzying heights of success have been achieved, you take little time to relax and enjoy the view, as you once again scan the horizon for new peaks to climb. You are serious and disciplined, with a strong need to have your life organized. You like to have a long-term destination, so that you know where you are going and why.

You are patient and cautious, possessing a down-to-earth nature that is involved with both the practical and material sides of life.

For many Capricorns, a career is all-important, and your self-worth often stems from gaining status and respect in your particular field. This desire to prove yourself means that great hardship can be endured for the sake of achieving your goal. Financial security is a prime concern, and your resources are managed with prudence and wisdom. You obtain real satisfaction from watching the slow-but-inexorable growth of your business affairs.

▲ Capricorn is associated with The Devil in tarot, which represents subservience and bad behavior, but also respite and release.

▶ This depiction of Capricorn features in a folio from an ancient Persian manuscript (no. 373), currently held by the Wellcome Trust.

TRADITIONAL ASSOCIATIONS

Capricorns are most closely associated with the following:

COLORS:	Shades of gray and brown
COUNTRIES:	India, Afghanistan
TAROT CARD:	Number 15, The Devil
FLOWERS:	Hellebore
BIRTHSTONE:	Jet, onyx
ANIMALS:	Goats, bears, bats
OCCUPATIONS:	Antique dealer, real estate agent, systems analyst, archaeologist
HERBS:	Comfrey
TREES:	Yew, pine
CITIES:	Brussels, Delhi, Oxford
FOOD:	Meat and salted nuts

Capricorns are responsible, with high moral standards and a mature outlook. You are at heart a traditionalist, and prefer sticking to well-worn paths and established social mores. Fear of public embarrassment means that you are reluctant to deviate from the norm. This unwillingness to experiment and take risks can halt the flow of progress in all areas of your life, but you are also blessed with a wry sense of humor, and deep sensuality that revels in earthly delights. You gain happiness from having the courage to listen and respond to the many different levels of your being.

THE CAPRICORN MAN

The typical Capricorn man has a well-developed frame with a strong jaw and defined features, and bright, knowing eyes. Beards are common when young, and a serious and slightly grim expression may be worn, which relaxes with age. You tend to walk with nimble steps, as though picking your way across a stony path.

You seem to have a maturity beyond your actual years, and for some Capricorn men, the youthful part of life is a real trial. You feel more comfortable with adults, and relish the chance to get out into the world. From an early age, ambitions are uppermost in your mind, and you do not let go until you have gained a secure foothold in your desired career.

Capricorn men are modest and self-effacing, preferring to stay behind the scenes while honors are given elsewhere. Even if your work has attained lasting glory, you avoid publicity, content instead with inner fulfillment and the recognition of your peers. You have a warm and reserved personality that mellows with age like a fine wine. A secure romance does much to temper your gruff manner, and helps you to overcome emotional isolation. Many of you are prepared to study hard in order to gain recognition and success in the eyes of the world.

▲ Although poisonous, the hellebore flower is considered in various cultures to have protective qualities.

THE CAPRICORN WOMAN

Capricorn women tend to have small, well-proportioned bodies with fine bones and classic beauty. Your eyes are sensuous and intriguing. You are conscious of your appearance, and dress with dignity and pride. Like the men, your face reflects sobriety in youth, and lightens up with age.

Capricorns are self-possessed, and you have the determination and focus to succeed. Once your heart and mind have set a course, potential difficulties are brushed aside by your rock-solid focus. Your energy is often geared toward ascending the ladder at work to reach a position of status and respect. You work hard to present an image of stability to the outside world, and disguise whatever troubles you are going through. Capricorn women sometimes encounter quite harsh fates, yet are capable of shouldering heavy burdens without complaining. You have a built-in sense of duty and obligation, and must be careful not to shut out potential happiness by accepting unnecessary strife. Your personal desires are sacred, and have every right to be fulfilled. A close relationship allows you to open up and receive much-needed love and support.

▲ Jet is associated with purification of negative energy and protection.

DRESS SENSE

Capricorn men and women have an essentially conservative approach to fashion. You shy away from unconventionality, preferring instead to go for formal, modest, and appropriate outfits. When buying clothes, you are motivated by price, quality, and durability, and pay little attention to short-term trends.

An austere streak means a few of you will wear clothes until they really wear out, but most Capricorns are anxious to maintain a smart and respectable image. Your thriftiness makes you hunt for a bargain before parting with precious cash, but work clothes are an exception, and you are prepared to spend big in order to make an impression that furthers your aims.

At the office, Capricorn women look good in sober dress suits that have an aura of efficiency and calm. You are drawn to dark tones of gray and brown, with occasional greens lightening the mood. Patent-leather shoes are popular, and executive-type briefcases lend an air of sophistication. For leisure wear, you avoid sloppy, unstylish garments and enjoy relaxing in designer casuals. A romantic evening provides the perfect setting for you to dazzle in a classic suit or little black dress. Jewelry completes the effect.

LIFESTYLE CHOICES

When choosing a home, Capricorns are guided by their respect for tradition and status. For you, property is a serious investment, and a wonderful opportunity to increase your social status. Living out in the country is immensely appealing, but the rigors of a modern career mean

HEALTH

CAPRICORNS like to work hard, and this can lead to stress-related problems. You thrive on a certain amount of pressure, but have difficulty knowing when to stop. When run down, your weakened immune system makes minor complaints hard to shift, and unreleased tension can prevent a good night's sleep. As most Capricorns possess a very strong constitution, a little moderation usually ensures marvelous levels of health.

The main body parts related to your sign are the knees, teeth, and bones. Advancing years can produce stiffness in the joints, and this is exacerbated by sedentary living or dampness. You are vulnerable to cavities, and may be a familiar patient at the dentist's. Always take scrupulous care of your teeth.

Capricorns can become very melancholic, with depression gradually seeping into your bones until every day is gray and morose. This can bring about chronic fatigue, and it's important for you to recognize when your spirits are getting low so you can get your life back on an even keel.

Capricorns are very tough on the whole, and face serious disease with a stoic fortitude; usually, your endurance wins through in the end.

▲ This 18-century depiction of Capricorn is one of a series of zodiacal signs at the impressive Jantar Mantar astronomical observatory, Jaipur, India.

you either reside in a city or suburb. If it is more economical, you prefer to buy a home of your own, as this seems much wiser to you than wasting money on rent. You have an astute sense for market trends, and will wait until a favorable time to buy. Strong links to your family mean that inherited properties are always cherished.

Capricorns like grand old houses and apartments, with spacious, well-proportioned rooms. If possible, you reside in the best neighborhoods, and at the very least, the immediate vicinity must be respectable. You prefer conventional furnishings, with subdued color schemes for the decor. Capricorns enjoy looking after family heirlooms, and these are frequently displayed alongside more recently acquired antiques.

Capricorns feel very relaxed within their own domain, and visitors are always treated as honored guests. Once you have invited someone to your home for a meal, you will undoubtedly provide a most memorable occasion.

You have excellent money-management skills that enable you to plan far into the future in anticipation of your needs. Saving comes naturally, and you are horrified at the thought of frivolous spending. Sometimes a spartan lifestyle is the result of too much fear, and you hoard your cash for no good reason.

Capricorns are not inclined to take risks, and when it comes to choosing the most appropriate way to invest, you check out expert advice and look for steady,

EXERCISE

WORK-OBSESSED Capricorns can spend far too much time slumped behind a desk. As a result many of them end up creating a sluggish body and a dull, passive mind. In order to overcome this, you should try to work out before getting down to paperwork. While many Capricorns have to fight an aversion to regular exercise, the rewards of finding something you can enjoy are great.

Keep your joints limbered with long walks (right), jogging, and gentle stretching. Yoga will also help you to relax. For more challenging sport activities, hiking and rock climbing give you a chance to see the beauty of mountains and hills, places where you feel very much at home. Capricorns benefit from being with nature.

long-term gains. You are innately patient, and are very skeptical of get-rich-quick schemes. You are prepared to work exceptionally hard in order to achieve some measure of financial freedom, sometimes enduring harsh conditions while you pave your way to success.

Many Capricorns are attracted by investment plans that take years, even decades, to mature. You have a talent for slow empire-building, and over time, may amass a considerable fortune. The stock market is a possible source of profit for you, and many Capricorns show a talent for business, growing into powerful, prominent tycoons.

CAPRICORNS AT PLAY

Leisure is not a priority for industrious Capricorns. Career always comes first with you, and even spare hours are often spent boosting its progress. Some people fail to appreciate that you actually enjoy working hard, and can find it difficult to get involved in activities that, to you, seem to be wasting your time.

When your job is going well, however, you are more inclined to indulge in relaxing pursuits. Capricorns have a reserved, reflective psyche, and you like to unwind with a thought-provoking book. Museums satisfy an interest in the past, and you can become something of an amateur historian.

You are attracted to formal study and training that have useful qualifications, and enjoy socializing in academic settings. Evening classes meet your creative needs, and you have a penchant for pottery and art. Many Capricorns are home-maintenance enthusiasts, as you possess both practical hands and a desire to economize. Friends are very important and you make every effort to stay in touch. You celebrate your work triumphs in style, usually inviting everyone to toast your success.

You have a strong sense of modesty, and dislike being thrust into the limelight, especially if you are on unfamiliar ground. Capricorns respect tradition and the status quo, and feel threatened by radical, anarchistic views. New ideas can at first be rejected on principle.

You conduct yourself with dignity, anxious to avoid any public humiliation. Your personal feelings are private, and not for public knowledge. Capricorns need to feel rooted to the past, and will delight in passing on something worthwhile to future generations.

THE PERFECT LOVE MATCH

Discover how Capricorns fare in relationships with other star signs

Aries	Childish	❤❤
Taurus	Deep love	❤❤❤❤❤
Gemini	Keep walking!	❤
Cancer	Perfect partners	❤❤❤❤❤
Leo	Surprisingly possible	❤❤❤
Virgo	The earth moves	❤❤❤❤❤
Libra	Forget it	❤❤
Scorpio	Intense but good	❤❤❤❤
Sagittarius	Restless nonevent	❤
Capricorn	Mountaintop delight	❤❤❤❤❤
Aquarius	Complementary	❤❤❤
Pisces	Sublime romance	❤❤❤❤❤

AQUARIUS JANUARY 20–FEBRUARY 18

Aquarians have a strong independent spirit that longs to break free from the restrictions imposed by conventional ideas. You are idealistic and innovative, replacing old and outdated thinking with fresh perspectives. Strongly drawn toward humanitarian issues, you experiment to discover your true identity. Aquarians are nonconformists on the whole, and are not afraid to break away from convention. You are determined to follow your principles, even if this means shunning considered opinion and forging ahead on your own.

Rebelling against the crowd gives you something to fight, and you possess a deep-rooted need to reform the status quo.

You tend to explore many visionary concepts, which only time may judge. Some are later dismissed as mere eccentricity while a few will preempt future trends with an illuminating flash of genius. Aquarians obtain a perverse satisfaction in rejecting established values, even when these have inherent worth. With maturity, you learn to separate the wheat from the chaff, and understand changing cycles in light of history.

▲ Aquarius is associated with The Star card in tarot, which represents bright prospects, hope, new opportunities, and success gained from hard work.

▶ A detail from a celestial map depicting the constellation of Aquarius. In this example, the sign is portrayed as a male figure.

LE CAPRICORNE
L'AEROSTAT
LE MICROSCOPE
LE VERSEAU
LE POISSON AUSTRAL
Fomalhaut
à l'horizon
LA GRUE
L'ATELIER DE

TRADITIONAL ASSOCIATIONS

Aquarians are most closely associated with the following:

COLORS:	Electric blues and greens
COUNTRIES:	Russia, Poland, Croatia
TAROT CARD:	Number 17, The Star
FLOWERS:	Snowdrop
BIRTHSTONE:	Aquamarine, amethyst
ANIMALS:	Peacocks
OCCUPATIONS:	Scientist, care-giver, electronic engineer, astrologist
HERBS:	Mandrake
TREES:	Rowan, mountain ash
CITIES:	Los Angeles
FOOD:	Health and organic foods

In your search for utopia, you are prepared to go it alone. This contradiction makes personal relationships a challenge, and your inner detachment struggles with emotional commitment. Part of you desperately wants to be close, but you also want to stay free. It is not always easy to reconcile these opposing points of view. You have a global consciousness, and appreciate each culture for what it is. Aquarians vehemently oppose prejudice, and you are deeply stirred by social injustice and oppression. This concern with humanity allows you to recognize that the individual is responsible for the whole.

THE AQUARIAN MAN

The Aquarian man tends to be fairly tall, with lithe limbs and strong bones. You often appear deep in thought, and when your interest is aroused, your eyes sparkle and your brows rise. You walk quickly unless you are deep in thought, when your steps can be irregular, and your head is slightly lowered.

Aquarians must express their originality and you are attracted to experiences and concepts that help you to solidify your sense of self. By being prepared to leave tradition behind, you find out what you really believe in, and how to utilize your unique perceptions.

You are fascinated by alternative ways of living, and how modern technology can be used to heal the planet. Aquarians have a scientific bent, and you combine this with a sharp intuition to reason and probe new frontiers of thought. Your emotions may be sublimated by logic, and your cool persona can make you appear to be rather offhand. But once you find your mission, life has tremendous focus and clarity.

For Aquarian men, a loving union is the ultimate test, and provides you with the opportunity to reveal your soul.

▲ The very first flowers of spring, snowdrops are said to represent hope and new beginnings.

THE AQUARIAN WOMAN

The typical Aquarian woman has a large bone structure and a well-proportioned face. You have clear, lively eyes that dart back and forth, with a fresh complexion and an open disposition. If you become excited, your arms tend to move about frantically, and your whole body takes on an electric presence.

Aquarians have an essentially unpredictable nature. Your feelings are prone to change without warning, which can cause confusion. At times you yearn for close and intimate company; then, out of the blue, a sense of claustrophobia descends, and you withdraw to seek solace alone.

As life progresses, you are able to stay centered while the pendulum swings, and this brings you growing confidence and peace. Aquarian women are strongly attuned to the earth and to people, and you enjoy being involved with small and large communities, often supporting groups that aim to improve others' lives. Aquarian women must follow the dictates of their conscience, and you will only be happy when you have discovered how to live by your principles. You long to find a partner who can accept your independence and understand your emotional shifts.

▲ Characteristics associated with aquarmarine include courage.

DRESS SENSE

Aquarians have an individualistic approach to fashion, and you resist slavishly pursuing current trends, unless they really catch your eye. You can be quite experimental with your choice of clothes, and are attracted to styles that have originality and flair. Some Aquarians are very daring and happily flirt with outrageous, avant-garde designs, but most of you are more modest, limiting yourself to an audacious use of color.

You are often seduced by images that spring from social movements. These outfits embody the ideas of the time, and you sometimes cling to these styles, even if they have ceased to be relevant—Aquarians can be extremely rigid in this way. Both sexes recoil from faceless conformity and if forced to wear a uniform as part of your work, you like to wear accessories to maintain your individuality.

Women have a vivid sense of color, and are especially drawn to vibrant turquoise blues and greens. Purple is also popular. You prefer jobs that allow freedom of expression, and select garments that are comfortable and harmonize with your moods. Smooth, silky textures are favored, and when dressing up, you exude glamour.

Aquarian men are less eccentric dressers, but still display a marked defiance of convention. You feel relaxed in casuals, and feel much more at ease in these, whatever the demands of the situation.

LIFESTYLE CHOICES

Your experimental lifestyles can produce some unusual homes. Aquarians are often interested in sharing property with others, and for some time you may avoid living alone. It makes you feel secure to be part of a group, and you enjoy the sense

HEALTH

YOUR hectic lifestyle may preclude sufficient exercise to ensure good health. Aquarians have intense minds that seek plenty of stimulation, but you are not always so in tune with your body's needs. Lack of movement on a daily basis constricts energy and hinders the circulatory system.

In winter months, numbness in the hands and feet can develop into swelling if not kept in check. In extreme instances, you have difficulty adjusting to both hot and cold weather. A sensible physical regime ensures that you are able to maintain your internal equilibrium.

The ankles are linked to the sign of Aquarius, and are prone to twists and sprains. You should be extra careful when playing sports, and make an effort to wear appropriate shoes. You are resilient, and take most minor complaints in your stride. On the rare occasions that serious disease penetrates your defenses, you may be opposed to conventional medicine, preferring instead to trust your recovery to alternative treatments.

These usually prove effective, and seem to suit your particular constitution. Aquarians are also subject to sudden ills that vanish without a trace.

A detail from Gerard Mercator's celestial globe of 1551, showing the constellation of Aquarius. The globe is on show in the Harvard Map Collection.

of collective responsibility. Some idealistic Aquarians live in bohemian New Age communes, and are great believers in housing cooperatives. You are idealistic, and happy to help out friends who have nowhere to stay.

You hold no allegiance to a particular location, and appreciate the merits of both the country and the city. Aquarians prefer their residence to be spacious and airy, with plenty of natural light. You are fastidious about clutter, as this imbues a feeling of constriction. The general ambience you create is cool and fresh, with striking, imaginative colors. Finances permitting, you indulge a passion for gadgets and technology to create an up-to-date and perhaps cutting-edge abode. A sparse use of furniture complements the mood.

As the years go by, it becomes increasingly important for you to have a home of your own. Because of your principles, this can be hard to admit.

Aquarians are not motivated by a desire to make vast fortunes. If one of your brilliant ideas catches on, riches may indeed result and you can welcome that, but you are more concerned with communicating your vision, and take little comfort from material gain. Whatever you do must find accord with your altruistic stance. Aquarians are strongly advised to seek expert advice before trying to get one of their more radical or eccentric schemes off the ground. This will avoid many potential pitfalls and disasters.

EXERCISE

MODEST amounts of walking, jogging, swimming, and cycling do much to keep an Aquarian's blood flowing and the joints supple. If you pick a fun activity that is easy to integrate regularly into your lifestyle, the transformation to increased fitness will come relatively painlessly!

Dancing (right) gives you the chance to express yourself physically, and most Aquarians find that they have a good sense of rhythm and a natural ease with sound. Aquarians also enjoy skiing, as you relish good clean air and the healthful environment of a mountainous landscape.

In order to stretch both body and mind, the eastern disciplines of aikido and t'ai chi give you a good insight into the nature of energy.

While you are so absorbed with other areas of your life, your finances may be neglected. You dislike being hemmed in by a lack of cash, so you usually make an effort to be self-sufficient. Aquarians are resourceful, and if pushed, you dig up some fairly unorthodox ways to earn money. The harsh reality of debt eventually teaches you to curb your extravagant tendencies. Aquarians are not greedy, and many keep their savings in a basic account. Ethical investments appeal, as you like to know where your money is going and what it will be used for. Whatever your level of wealth, this is generously shared with family and friends.

The strong humanitarian side of the Aquarian nature shows itself in many practical ways, and you enjoy making donations to favorite charities.

AQUARIANS AT PLAY

Aquarians like to pursue eclectic interests in their leisure time. You enjoy studying, and can find New Age topics very inspiring. One aspect of this field may grow into a consuming hobby, or possibly a future career. Aquarians are always receptive to ideas on the cutting edge of science and culture.

Your social circle is likely to consist of unusual individuals, united by their free-thinking and unconventional approach to life. To an outsider, this assortment may appear disparate. Thought-provoking plays and movies appeal, especially if they concern issues close to your heart. You are interested in parties, but your capricious moods mean it's hard to predict whether you will actually turn up!

Aquarians appreciate shared company, but you are also reluctant to pin yourself down with too many commitments. Sometimes you refuse an invitation purely to keep your options open. You often decide to visit a friend on a whim.

Aquarians dislike being forced to conform—you are intrigued by the concept of a global village. If you really feel stifled, you behave rebelliously. You have a soft spot for futuristic technology, and are often among the first to acquire the latest executive toy. Aquarians hate getting stuck in a rut, and when this happens, you are open to being freed by sudden and exciting events. You enjoy persuading others to change their minds, but are yourself somewhat inflexible. Aquarians are usually pacifists, and you recoil from the thought of violence.

THE PERFECT LOVE MATCH

Discover how Aquarius fares in relationships with other star signs

Aries	Exciting love	❤❤❤❤
Taurus	Uninspiring	❤❤❤
Gemini	Heaven!	❤❤❤❤❤
Cancer	Disastrous	❤
Leo	Stubborn partners	❤❤❤
Virgo	You must be kidding!	❤
Libra	Fresh 'n' sweet	❤❤❤❤❤
Scorpio	Interesting...	❤❤❤
Sagittarius	Tops for passion	❤❤❤❤❤
Capricorn	Surprisingly possible	❤❤❤
Aquarius	True soul mates	❤❤❤❤❤
Pisces	Magnetic affair	❤❤❤

PISCES FEBRUARY 19–MARCH 20

Dreamy and sensitive, Pisceans are blessed with deep intuition and a wealth of emotion. You live in the world of feelings, and your mutable nature ebbs and flows in tune with an inner tide. Your imagination is so strong that, at times, it merges reality with fantasy. Pisceans need time to understand the true calling of their souls. Pisceans are kind and compassionate characters on the whole, with an empathy for their fellow human beings that makes it hard for you not to care for others even when their actions interfere with your own life.

As an individual, you are extremely open, and you sometimes feel like an emotional sponge, absorbing both positive and negative energy from those around you. This lack of boundaries may leave you feeling drained at times, and to recharge your delicate psyche, it is essential to rest a while in a tranquil, private setting.

Pisceans are vulnerable to losing their identity by pouring themselves into other people. Like a river seeking the sea, you were born with an instinct always to transcend yourself through merging with something greater.

▲ Pisces is associated with The Moon in tarot, which represents deception in others and trickery. It can also signify the overcoming of problems.

▶ A depiction of Pisces from the **Harley Aratus**, a collection of astrological texts ca 820–840, currently held at the British Library, London.

Pisces quorum alter paulo praelabitur ante
Et magis horrisonis aquilonis tangitur alis
Atque horum e caudis duplices uelut esse catenae
Dicesque diuersae per lumina serpunt
Atque una tamen in stella communiter haeret
Quem ueteres soliti caelestem dicere nodum
Andromedae leuo ex umero si quaerere perges
Adpositum poteris supra cognoscere piscem

PISCES

TRADITIONAL ASSOCIATIONS

Pisceans are most closely associated with the following:

COLORS:	Sea greens, violet
COUNTRIES:	Portugal, Samoa, Morocco
TAROT CARD:	Number 18, The Moon
FLOWERS:	Iris
BIRTHSTONE:	Pearl, moonstone
ANIMALS:	Fish, dolphins
OCCUPATIONS:	Dancer, healer, musician, artist, psychic
HERBS:	Evening primrose
TREES:	Willow, hazel
CITIES:	Lisbon, Seville, Venice
FOOD:	Fruit, vegetables with a high water content

This desire can take you across an ocean of experience from the divinity of mystical union to the degradation of alcoholic despair. Pisceans are capable of both these extremes as well as every shore that lies between.

You are often unsure about how you feel, and the resulting ambivalence can pull you in two very different directions. Which way you finally choose to swim is a test for your wisdom and strength of character—your destiny is usually negotiable.

On occasions your sensitivity may make life painful and difficult. You may be tempted to escape, but by facing these challenges courageously, you can trawl up treasures from the deep. Pisceans are credited with being romantic, creative, and full of love. They have a potential for great happiness and lasting joy.

THE PISCEAN MAN

The average Piscean man has a slightly bulbous head, with eyes that are set well back, seeming to gaze at distant horizons. Your shoulders are prominent, and you walk a bit like a sailor, with a pronounced rolling gait. Your eyebrows are often thick, and your face is very mutable, conveying a variety of expressions that change with your mood.

There is no doubt that you are a natural romantic, determined to pursue as many of your dreams as possible. The amazing Piscean imagination is certainly able to achieve the fantastic and unbelievable, but occasionally you discover that you are, in fact, only chasing pipe dreams. And a refusal to acknowledge reality, even when it is obvious, can produce little more than empty musing.

The Piscean man is very emotional, and you are more sensitive than you care to admit to others. You employ your formidable intuition to dodge problems, rather than tackling them head-on. This softness of approach is one of your greatest assets, and allows you to elude danger and maximize opportunity.

Pisceans like to have romance and intrigue in their lives, and when involved in a good relationship, you view life through rose-tinted glasses. Your heart longs for such a loving union.

▲ Characteristics associated with the iris include faith, hope, wisdom, courage, and admiration.

THE PISCEAN WOMAN

The typical Piscean woman is slim when younger, but tends to hold water and put on weight with age. You have a moon-shaped face, with mysterious eyes and an alluring smile. After a hard day you look exhausted, and any current worries show up in your expression. When relaxed, you are radiant and serene.

Piscean women have nebulous feelings that produce confusing extremes of elation and disappointment. You are sometimes at the mercy of these emotions, which threaten to engulf your fragile sense of self. Experience teaches you that by surrendering to the flow of your watery nature, you survive intact, with renewed faith.

▲ Moonstone is said to bring abundance to one's life.

It is vital that you should share your emotional life by talking with friends, even releasing tears if required. You are very loving and considerate, finding it hard to refuse if someone asks you for help. You are susceptible to outside influences, and have difficulty seeing yourself in a positive light. Maturity brings increased perspective and confidence.

Piscean women have a soft, vulnerable image that belies their inner fortitude. You yearn for a strong, supportive partner who appreciates the depth of your love and also has the sensitivity to respond.

DRESS SENSE

Pisceans have a quiet magnetism that adds a glamorous touch to the most humble outfits. Your clothes tend to reflect how things are going in your life, and when times are hard or you are disorganized, you may lack the energy to take care of your appearance. Pisceans are naturally drawn to shimmering colors, evocative textures, and romantic images far removed from mundane drabness. You gladly spend money to achieve your desired look, and your wardrobe is a testimony to your ever-changing lifestyle and nature.

At work, women wear sensible, but feminine, skirts and dresses. You are well aware of your attractiveness to the opposite sex, and use this in many subtle ways. Soft, comfortable casuals are your favorite choice for hanging around, and you enjoy relaxing without makeup. For a special night out, you emulate Cinderella at the ball, resplendent in a beautiful, magical dress, with matching shoes and subtle perfume to evoke passion and intrigue.

Piscean men may feel slightly awkward in a suit, as you are generally more at ease in casual clothes with fluid, stylish lines. You love wearing the sea colors, and for a special dinner or night out, will dazzle with astute grooming and romantic panache.

LIFESTYLE CHOICES

The Piscean abode provides a safe harbor from the harsh environment of the outside world. Privacy and tranquillity are

HEALTH

PISCEANS' sensitive constitution means your health is directly influenced by how you are feeling. When you are emotionally drained, you are subject to a variety of minor ills that are often psychosomatic. It is important to listen to your subconscious, as you can gain useful insight into which situations to avoid.

With more serious illnesses, you tend to give in to them, letting them wash over you until they finally recede. For a Piscean, this is by far the quickest route to recovery. Friends and family support you in this, and your fighting spirit is stimulated by their love. When suffering from severe stress, some Pisceans are prone to seek relief through alcohol and drugs. With this in mind, your inclination toward addiction should make you extremely moderate when indulging in social pleasures of this kind.

The feet are the main body part relating to Pisces, and you may suffer from corns, warts, bunions, and swelling. It is imperative that you wear comfortable, roomy shoes with good support. In winter, a gentle foot massage with a stimulating oil can enhance circulation and help keep your feet in good condition.

absolutely vital, and give you a chance to unwind and release any built-up stress. Pisceans love to live by water, and you really appreciate the soothing beauty of the sea. Cities are exciting, but the sheer mass of humanity can tax your joie de vivre.

Even if you live in a concrete jungle, your apartment's interior will have an overriding gentle and relaxing atmosphere. When choosing somewhere to live, you are guided by gut feelings, and can easily visualize its appearance after decorating and furnishing.

Pisceans like to be surrounded by rich colors and fabrics that create a full-bodied, emotive mood. Your attachment to accumulated possessions means this flotsam and jetsam can create some interesting scenery. You give rooms real character when you adorn them with personal items, paintings, and houseplants.

▲ Detail showing a planet in the house of Pisces, from the horoscope in **The Book of the Birth of Iskandar** (1411).

The general impression you give is warm and welcoming, though sometimes a little cluttered. Pisceans are sensitive hosts, and always make guests feel relaxed and at home.

Pisceans' unworldly streak may make it hard for you to get to grips with personal finance. You must make a real effort to focus on annoying details in order to keep your head above water; it is true that some careless Pisceans lurch from one financial disaster to another.

You are generous in the extreme, and can be easily moved by a sob story. Make sure your own needs are well taken care of before you start administering to

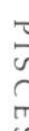

EXERCISE

PISCEANS absolutely love water, and swimming is always a natural choice for exercise. Not only does it tone the body, but it also peacefully releases tension—something you benefit from tremendously. Having said that, you sometimes find overcrowded, noisy environments completely insufferable, and would rather go for a quiet, solitary walk (right), preferably in woodland or open countryside.

Mental relaxation is vital for Pisceans, and yoga offers gentle stretching that soothes your mind. With regular practice, you may achieve new levels of emotional balance, and for many Pisceans, yoga is the perfect antidote to stress. Ballet and dance appeal to your romantic nature, and you find the music uplifting.

others. You enjoy spending funds to have a fulfilling life; because you are not very materialistic, following your heart is more important than acquiring riches. Provided you have enough to live comfortably, you are generally quite content.

Some Pisceans are seduced by the glamour of wealth, and may be exploited by unscrupulous people, who talk you into making dubious investments. Your fertile imagination can lead you astray, so before actually parting with any hard cash, you should seek the advice of a reputable expert. Pisceans benefit from learning to save, and thus creating a useful buffer against any future adversity.

PISCEANS AT PLAY

Your leisure hours are very precious, as you often find day-to-day existence a strain. When really tired, many Pisceans enjoy curling up with a good book or a long session in front of the TV. It is not unusual for you to take a refreshing nap, and you love the feeling of having absolutely nothing to do.

Pisceans are generally very artistically inclined. Your superb imagination can find expression through painting, music, and writing, among other disciplines. Fantasy and myth are popular themes for you to explore and you may enjoy studying these in an evening class or group.

You love your many friends dearly, and relish the time you are able to spend together. Intimate dinners in, and colorful nights out, give you a chance to catch up on the latest gossip and share your life with others. With company, it is even harder for you to resist indulging your sweet tooth and passion for wine!

For a big night out, you tend to like movies, the theater, and glamorous, intriguing parties—Pisceans need a touch of romance and magic in all they do.

Pisceans love walking by the sea at sunset, allowing their thoughts to drift with the tide. Sometimes your spirit cries out for nature, and you simply have to get out of the city for a short break in more peaceful surroundings. If you feel life is drab and gray, every once in a while you need to make a temporary escape.

Being forced to be too logical and rational can make you depressed at times. Pisceans are very much creatures of emotion, and you don't like feeling too cut off and detached. You are a very private person, and find it difficult to cope with situations requiring exposure.

THE PERFECT LOVE MATCH

Discover how Pisceans fare in relationships with other star signs

Aries	Impulsive and forceful	♥♥
Taurus	Secure loving	♥♥♥♥
Gemini	Superficial	♥
Cancer	Sweet 'n' deep	♥♥♥♥♥
Leo	Short-term fizzler	♥♥♥
Virgo	Pragmatic partner	♥♥♥♥
Libra	Once in a while	♥♥♥
Scorpio	Yes!	♥♥♥♥♥
Sagittarius	Steamy affair	♥♥♥
Capricorn	Rock-solid lover	♥♥♥♥♥
Aquarius	Unstable attraction	♥♥
Pisces	Ultimate romance	♥♥♥♥♥

INDEX

PICTURE CREDITS

Every effort has been made to list the copyright holders of the images in this book. Any omissions will be amended in future editions of the work.

Alamy Stock Photo: p. 24 The Art Archive; pp. 46r, 54r, 62r, 70r, 78r, 86r, 94r, 102r, 110r, 126r, 134r Ben Molyneux; pp. 63, 95 SuperStock; p. 118r Greg Balfour Evans
Corbis Images: p. 7 The Gallery Collection; p. 10 Gianni Dagli Orti; p. 13 Pascal Deloche/ Godong; p. 14 Leemage; p. 17: Heritage Images; pp. 44, 67, 99 Stapleton Collection; p. 45; p. 47 Werner Forman/Werner Forman Archive/Werner Forman
Shutterstock: p. 4 and throughout Morphart Creation; p. 6 Avella; pp. 8–9 Marzolino; pp. 11, 40–1, 127 yoshi0511; p. 12 Kokhanchikov; p. 15 Peter Hermes Furian; pp. 20–1 Slanapotam; pp. 22–4 aiym design; pp. 27–38 animicsgo; p. 39 vladm; p. 42 MiSt21; pp. 46l, 54l, 62l, 70l, 78l, 86l, 94l, 102l, 110l, 118l, 126l, 134l xenia_ok; p. 49t Arevka; p. 49b Tarzhanova; p. 52 Vixit; p. 57t Zhanna Smolyar; pp. 57b, 121b Vitalii Tiagunov; p. 60 Gomita; p. 65t lynea; p. 65b ChinellatoPhoto; p. 68 arek_malang; p. 73t wacomka; p. 73b Africa Studio; p. 76 Monkey Business Images; p. 81t Zenina Anastasia; p. 81b Dekdoyjaidee; p. 84 Iakov Filimonov; p. 88t Marina Grau; p. 88b Nastya22; p. 92 Val Thoermer; p. 97t Sharon Freeman; p. 97b nadi555; p. 100 Jack Z Young; p. 105t Azurhino; p. 105b cvalle; p. 108 Flashon Studio; p. 113t stasia_ch; p. 113b Tarzhanova; p. 116 Maridav; p. 121t ein Nouwens; p. 124 DUSAN ZIDAR; p. 129t svemar; p. 129b Boykung; p. 132 AlexSutula; p. 137t Michael Vigliotti; p. 137b Vladimir Kovalchuk; p. 140 Petar Paunchev.
Wikimedia Commons: p. 26 Vassil; pp. 51, 75, 123 Yann Forget; pp. 55, 131 Micheletb/Harvard Map Collections (CC-PD-Mark); pp. 59, 87 Jean-Pol GRANDMONT; p. 71 Adam Cuerde/ Library of Congress; p. 79 Hugo Grotius (CC0); p. 83 Sławomir Pastuszka; p. 91 Zde; ; pp. 103, 107, 115, 119, 139 Wellcome Library, London; pp. 111, 135 British Library.